Apologetics and the Biblical Christ

Woodstock Papers

Occasional Essays for Theology

PREPARED BY

Professors of the Faculty of Theology
Woodstock College, Woodstock, Maryland

EDITED BY

JOHN COURTNEY MURRAY, S.J.
WALTER J. BURGHARDT, S.J.

No. 6

THE NEWMAN PRESS
WESTMINSTER, MARYLAND
1963

APOLOGETICS

and the

BIBLICAL CHRIST

by Avery Dulles, S.J.

Professor of Fundamental Theology
Woodstock College

THE NEWMAN PRESS

WESTMINSTER, MARYLAND

1963

Imprimi Potest: JOHN M. DALEY, S.J.
Praep. Prov. Marylandiae

Nihil Obstat: JOSEPH ZALOTAY
Censor Deputatus

Imprimatur: LAWRENCE J. SHEHAN, D.D.
Archbishop of Baltimore

February 28, 1963

The *nihil obstat* and *imprimatur* are official declarations that a book or pamphlet is free of doctrinal and moral error. No implication is contained therein that those who have granted the *nihil obstat* and *imprimatur* agree with the opinions expressed.

Copyright © 1963 by The Missionary Society of Saint Paul the Apostle
in the State of New York

Library of Congress Catalog Card Number: 63–22027

Printed in the United States of America

Cover photo "The Glory of Christ" (Basilica of Vezelay) from the book *Christ's Image* (Tudor Publishing Co.).

⋆ Contents ⋆

★ Introduction ★

In July, 1961, I was asked to deliver five lectures at the Summer Biblical Institute for Priests at Glen Ellyn, Ill., dealing with the impact of modern biblical studies on Christian apologetics. The five chapters of this book are, with minor revisions, the lectures then given. They do not pretend to offer more than a rough sketch of the problems and answers, but even a sketch can sometimes be of service. It can at least open up new perspectives.

In presenting these lectures to a wider public, and without the opportunity for oral discussion which was provided in the question period following each of the talks, I am aware of the possibility that certain statements may give rise to difficulties or misunderstandings. Indeed, this seems almost inevitable, granted the wide scope of the book, its brevity, and the variety of background and point of view which may be expected among the readers. Nevertheless, I believe that I have made my general argument clear enough to be intelligible to those who attentively follow my whole presentation. Such difficulties as still remain after a careful reading of this work may be an effective stimulus to further reading and study. Hoping that some will be so inclined, I have given a few bibliographical indications at the end of each chapter.

For the general reader, I should perhaps clarify in this introduction one distinction taken for granted in the body of the book: that between the Catholic understanding of the Bible and biblical apologetics. In his reading of the Bible, the

Catholic believer quite rightly relies on all the positive helps afforded by his faith. He accepts the inspiration and inerrancy of Scripture as the Church understands these; he draws upon his general knowledge of the Christian revelation, and in the exegesis of particular passages he is rightly influenced by the interpretation which has been given to them in Catholic tradition and Church documents. Thanks to these helps, the Catholic reader of the New Testament finds more in its pages than would be apparent to an unbeliever. He will understand the Gospels as describing the Incarnation of the Son of God, His virginal conception at Nazareth, His birth at Bethlehem, in the days of Caesar Augustus. He will look upon Jesus as a person truly and literally divine, and will be satisfied that He gathered disciples, instructed them in the kingdom of God, promised them certain powers within the Church, and guaranteed to this same Church the unfailing assistance of the Holy Spirit till the end of time. In the New Testament, moreover, the Catholic reader finds perfect assurance that Jesus worked numerous and astounding miracles, that He instituted the Holy Eucharist, that He was betrayed by one of the Twelve, that He suffered, died on the cross, and rose corporeally from the dead, that He appeared repeatedly to His disciples, and finally, after a period of some forty days, was seen to ascend into heaven. There is no reason why any of the faithful, reading the New Testament, should feel doubts about the reality of these events. Sound biblical scholarship has in no way impugned these fundamentals of Catholic belief.

If the Catholic then pauses to reflect on the motives for his conviction that all these events really occurred, he will easily see that he accepts them not simply because of his confidence in the Gospels as documents of scientific history, in

the sense that they would be so understood by modern un-
believers. Rather, he reads the Bible within the Church, according it that high authority which the Church assigns it,
and understanding it in harmony with the whole Catholic
community. The Catholic does not wish to find in the Scriptures any meaning other than that which the Church finds
in them. Without expecting magisterial pronouncements on
every disputed question, he will see the need for some authoritative guidance. When Church authorities, vigilant to pro-
tect the Scriptures from distortion, see fit to give authoritative
interpretations of particular texts—as is rather infrequently
done—the Catholic reader will accept these determinations
with the degree of inner and outer assent which may be required in the individual case. In all of this he will see
no arbitrary authoritarianism but a gracious disposition of
Providence for the better understanding of the Christian
revelation.

The Catholic apologist is, quite evidently, a believer. Like
any Catholic, he fully accepts the Christian message as understood by the Church. But as an apologist, he has a particular
function, namely, to show the reasonableness of the assent
of faith. This means that he cannot, in his work as an apologist, make use of all the helps which he enjoys as a believer.
He has to rely on purely human evidences. He cannot invoke
the "analogy of faith," deducing conclusions from the con-
tents of Christian revelation, since the acceptability of the
Christian faith is the precise point at issue. For the same reason, he cannot argue directly from Church regulations. Nor
can he assume that the Bible is a divinely inspired source,
free from error. In the pursuit of his trade, the apologist will
sometimes make concessions "for the sake of the argument"
which as a believer he does not make. Quite conceivably, for

instance, he might say as a believer that Christ clearly gave His apostles the power to forgive sins; and at the same time, as an apologist, he might treat this as a point not yet proved —or even as something not provable by direct evidences. When the apologist writes in this vein, the reader ought not to think that this implies a lack of conviction or loyalty on his part. It means simply that he is operating within the necessary limits of his discipline. He has to treat as questionable whatever he has not been able to establish by purely rational investigation.

The apologist has at his disposal a vast store of potential arguments for the reasonableness of his faith. He is by no means limited to reliance on the data provided by the New Testament. Some would feel that, because of the complex literary and historical problems surrounding the Gospels, the contemporary apologist ought to rely chiefly on proofs of a different character, such as the wonderful sublimity of the Christian message, the durability and expansion of the Christian religion, the innumerable miracles recorded in Church history, and the splendid fruits of Catholic sanctity.

One reason for this shyness toward the Bible as an apologetical source is undoubtedly the great crisis in scriptural scholarship which shook the Christian world in the course of the past hundred years, reaching its climax in the first decades of the present century. In this period the historical value of the Bible was hotly contested. As a result of these controversies, it has come to be admitted by scholars of all faiths—leaving aside a few diehard fundamentalists—that we do not have in the Bible, or even in the Gospels, fully scientific history. That is to say, we possess for the life of Jesus no such sources as an academic historian would require for, say, an authoritative biography of Woodrow Wilson or Franklin

Roosevelt. We have no public documents, no contemporary newspaper reports or their equivalent, no personal letters, no stenographic records of speeches and conversations. Instead, we possess only brief memorials—or, more accurately, Gospels—which emanated from two of Christ's apostles and from two disciples of the apostles, and were put into writing from thirty to seventy years after his death. Is it not a hazardous enterprise, some might ask, to seek to establish from such jejune and dubious sources the stupendous tidings which the Gospels claim to bring?

The objection seems impressive at first sight, but still, I am convinced, it is far from cogent. In spite of all the apparent difficulties, I think it possible to show that the narratives of the New Testament make a powerful, and in some ways decisive, contribution to the credibility of the Christian revelation. This claim does not hold simply for the naive reader, but for the scholar as well. Apologetics need not look on biblical research as an enemy, as if its sole tendency were to undermine the credibility of the faith. If recent research has overthrown certain arguments that were once highly valued, we may rejoice at being delivered from such illusions. But the new evidences with which scholarship has supplied us make it possible to construct new arguments which were not used, or insufficiently used, by the apologetics of a generation ago. Apologetics is, or should be, a progressive discipline.

So far as biblical apologetics is concerned, the storm center presently hovers over the notion of history. A generation ago history was rather rigidly defined in accordance with the methodology of a particular school. It was assumed that if the Gospels did not measure up to the norms of current historiography, they could not be historical in any genuine sense, that they must be relegated to the category of myth or legend, poetry or fiction. In our day it is widely recognized that the term "history" should be more flexibly defined. There is popular history and technical history, factual history and interpretive history, external history and personal history, secular history and religious history. In terms of dichotomies such as these, the question is not so much whether the Gospels are historical as what type of history they contain. What is gradually emerging, under the guidance of serious scholarship, is a new understanding of the biblical historical genera.

For a New Testament apologetic, these developments are of the greatest moment. Thanks to modern research, it can be confidently maintained—relying not on the devotion of blind faith but on the weight of the evidence—that the Gospels embody traditions of the highest value. Their testimony is excellently suited for conveying a genuine appreciation of who Jesus was and what He accomplished. In order not to be scandalized by the supposed shortcomings of these little books, we have only to study them more thoroughly. For him who knows how to read them, they hold unsuspected treasures. Generally speaking, the better we understand the Bible, the more impressive and convincing we shall find its testimony to the person and the deeds of Jesus Christ.

AVERY DULLES, S.J.

Apologetics and the Biblical Christ

★ 1 ★

The Apologetics of Historicism

During the past few decades biblical studies have made enormous progress. Rapid progress is an excellent thing, but it often brings in its train disorientation, doubt, and confusion. This unfortunate result has to some degree occurred as regards the apologetical value of the New Testament. The Church has always seen in the New Testament, especially in the Gospels, a firm historical guarantee of the fact of Christian revelation. But the direction which scriptural studies have taken since the advent of form criticism has tended to disturb the confidence of many readers. Believing Christians today are understandably concerned about whether it is now necessary to revise or even abandon those arguments for Christian credibility which our grandfathers and fathers, or even we ourselves, were accustomed to accept.

Those working in the field of apologetics cannot simply bury their heads in the sand. They must keep abreast of current biblical criticism and see what, if anything, needs to be revamped. Like many other persons concerned with the field, I have become convinced that the apologetics of a generation ago is not adequate for today's needs. But a rejuvenated apologetics will not be totally new. It will have to incorporate what is still valid in the older approach, presenting it in modern dress.

The task of apologetics is, I take it, to state in the clearest possible form the objective rational grounds for faith. As Catholics, we are sure of our faith. We are confident, too, that it is a fully reasonable act, in conformity with man's nature as a rational being. We know that God has deposited in history sufficient signs of credibility to make it unreasonable to doubt or deny the Christian claims.

But to be able to state in clear and accurate terms what the signs of credibility are, and to show just how they are connected with the truth of the revelation—that is the arduous task of apologetics. It is a never-ending task. Each generation uncovers new evidence and proposes new questions. The Christian apologist must try to master all the principal arguments of credibility within the reach of his own age and to meet, so far as he can, the difficulties and anxieties of his own contemporaries.

Quite naturally, then, each age has its own style of apologetics. A glance over the centuries will make this clear. The early Fathers argued against the Jews that the Messianic prophecies had been fulfilled in Christ. Against the pagans they tried to establish that Christianity delivered men from moral degradation and instilled the highest virtue. In the Middle Ages St. Thomas Aquinas sought to exhibit Christianity as the summit of wisdom: it perfectly agreed with all the findings of Aristotelian philosophy and afforded answers to many questions which pure philosophy was powerless to solve. In the Counter Reformation Catholic apologetics took a very different turn. Controversialists like Bellarmine and Canisius tried to show that the Bible, far from teaching Protestantism, was an armory of Catholic orthodoxy. During the Enlightenment Christian apologetics had to adapt itself to the objections of the Rationalists. Protestants and Catholics alike busied themselves with demonstrating that Christianity

[4]

was a solemn republication of the truths and laws contained in the great book of nature. In the early nineteenth century Romanticism evoked yet another brand of apologetics. Christians felt it necessary to show that their faith satisfied the deepest instincts of the human heart and fostered the highest aesthetic experience.

Toward the middle of the nineteenth century the intellectual climate changed once more. Positivism became the vogue and gave birth to the cult of history as an exact science. History was no longer conceived as a more or less fanciful reconstruction of the past, nor as a meditation on the lessons of man's collective experience, but as a technical discipline concerned with unearthing the past "as it had really been" —*wie es eigentlich gewesen,* according to the famous phrase of Leopold von Ranke. An effort was made to exclude from history all that was subjective and arbitrary, to make it as dispassionate and rigorous as physics or chemistry. Scientific history, moreover, was regarded as the sole legitimate tool for dealing with the human past. This exaggerated esteem for scientific, factual history is often termed "historicism."

Historicism did not take long to collide with Christian orthodoxy. Christianity was a religion which claimed to rest upon solid historical fact, namely, the life and teaching of Jesus of Nazareth. Could faith justify itself before the bar of academic history? Historians eagerly set about the task of inquiring what would result if dogmatic presuppositions were set aside and the Bible were analyzed by the same norms which applied to profane historical sources.

The results of this inquiry have been surveyed by Dr. Albert Schweitzer in his famous study, *The Quest of the Historical Jesus,* first published in 1906. In the late eighteenth century, he shows, Jesus was portrayed as an enlightened

teacher of God, virtue, and immortality. In the early nineteenth century the romantic imagination saw in Him a religious genius, exuding the poetry of God. The Hegelian ideal-
ists then tried to show that Christ had ushered in a new
stage in the evolution of man's religious consciousness. The
moralizing writers of the late nineteenth century, influenced
by Albert Ritschl, depicted Jesus as a teacher of Kantian
ethics. Toward the end of the century social revolutionaries
found in Jesus a protagonist of the poor and oppressed. And
after reproducing all these pictures, each proposed in the
name of pure history, Schweitzer finds courage to add his
own: the portrait of a deluded religious fanatic preaching
the imminent destruction of the universe. Such is Schweitzer's personal reconstruction of the "historical Jesus."

Christian polemics have hardly ever succeeded in rising
above the prevailing assumptions of a given age. Perhaps
this is just as well, at least for their practical success. In any
case, the apologetics of the early twentieth century accepted
the assumptions of historicism. There was no disposition to
deny that scientific history could derive from the Gospels an
accurate portrait of the real Jesus. But the apologists differed
from the naturalists in insisting that the Jesus of history—
the Jesus discoverable by sound historical method—was
neither an impostor nor a dreamer nor a moralizing human-
itarian nor a social revolutionary. He was none other than
the Christ of faith. Thus there developed an apologetics
which placed unquestioning confidence in the powers of
scientific historical method to defend the rational basis of the
Christian faith. This is what I call the "historicist apologetic."

For examples of historicist apologetics one might turn
to almost any of the theological manuals on revelation or the
polemical "lives of Jesus" written by Catholics in the first

[6]

three decades of the twentieth century. I shall choose for analysis the great two-volume work of Hilarin Felder, O.M.Cap., entitled *Christ and the Critics*. Published in German in 1911, it appeared in English in 1924. Schweitzer himself has paid tribute to Felder's prodigious command of the modern literature about Jesus.

After inspecting the nature of the assault being made upon Christian revelation, Felder states in his introductory chapter that apologetics must make use of strict historical method; otherwise it will not meet the attack. "Who is Christ?" he asks (Vol. 1, pp. 11–12):

Are the Gospel, the person, the doctrine, the life and deeds of Christ—that is to say, is *Christianity*—actual history? Did Christ declare himself to be really the Messiah and God, and did he furnish evidence for his Messiahship and deity? That is the one great *historical question* to which all others lead at last.

Only *by means of historical science* is this question to be answered, and only thus is the appearance of Jesus Christ and Christianity on this earth to be comprehended and explained.

Felder then lays down the rules of the game. In his apologetic, he asserts, he will not take for granted any of the mysteries of faith. He will call into question all the religious convictions of the biblical writers and study the Gospels as "merely historical documents treating of the life of Jesus" (1, 14). As apologists we must do so, for "if we summon the opponents of the Christian revelation before the bar of fair, unclouded history, we, on our side, must of course be equally scrupulous" (1, 13). "Only that method is historical which, without any previous assumption, examines the facts of Christianity, and supplements, or possibly corrects, one's own religious and philosophical opinions and views according to the result which has been historically established" (*ibid.*).

[7]

By this procedure Felder is confident that he can expose the vain pretensions of hostile criticism, which "is always boasting of its purely historical method" (1, 12). He will answer by showing on sheerly historical grounds "the *fact* that Christ represented himself as God, and his religion as divine, and that he undoubtedly furnished proofs for this assertion" (*ibid.*).

Let us take a brief look at the Christian demonstration proposed by Felder and the manuals of the same period. The argument falls into two sharply distinguished stages: the first is a consideration of the historical value of the Christian sources (especially the Gospels); the second, a proof from these sources that Jesus was Messiah and God.

How is it established that the Gospels are reliable historical sources? Their authors must be shown to be equipped with the necessary properties of any good witness: knowledge and truthfulness. By their knowledge is meant that they were in possession of the facts; by their truthfulness, that they intended to and did report them accurately.

In order to prove that the Evangelists knew the facts about Jesus, great weight was attached to the fact of strict authenticity, viz., that the four Evangelists were none other than Matthew the Apostle, John Mark, Luke the Physician, and John the Apostle. Once this is granted, the argument proceeds smoothly. We may quote from L. C. Fillion's *The Life of Christ* (St. Louis: Herder, 1928–29; Vol. 1, pp. 71 f.) on this point:

> As members of the Apostolic College, St. Matthew and St. John were close companions of the Savior for about three years, constantly seeing and hearing Him, being present at His preaching and miracles, living in intimate association with Him. . . . Though St. Mark and St. Luke did not have the privilege of being eye-witnesses, yet their

authority as historians of Christ was hardly less than that of the two Apostle-Evangelists. Having become the intimate disciples, respectively, of St. Peter and St. Paul, they faithfully reproduce the Apostles' preaching in their accounts. . . . They were witnesses by hearing.

The second qualification, the veracity of the Evangelists, is crucial for the historicist apologetics. Felder says that "perhaps the most important [question] of all" is whether "the sacred writers have, consciously or unconsciously, not written the true and actual history of Jesus, but have designed the portrait of Christ according to the standards of the belief of that time and with the embellishments characteristic of the period" (1, 10–11). "That sufficient attention has not been paid to this question in our apologetics handbooks and our larger works, anyone can easily convince himself" (1, 11).

The proof by which Felder, Fillion, and similar authors seek to establish that the Gospels are strict history is taken chiefly from certain assertions of the Evangelists, especially those found in the prologue to the third Gospel and in the epilogue to the fourth. The latter reads: "This is the disciple who bears witness concerning these things, and who has written these things, and we know that his witness is true" (21:24). On the basis of declarations such as this, Felder does not hesitate to assert: ". . . no possibility of doubt remains that these men wish themselves to be regarded as historians, and their writings as historically faithful representations" (1, 98). "The Evangelists, therefore, wish most conscientiously to report the historic truth about Jesus, his life, deeds and teaching. They write no line which they do not consider absolutely correct. They relate no episode in the life of Jesus, the actuality of which they do not believe" (1, 99; cf. 2, 372).

To these arguments of Felder one may add the observation of Fillion: "On reading the Gospels, and still more when meditating on them, one is promptly convinced that the writers are sincere, disinterested, faultlessly impartial. They tell their story simply, objectively, in a wholly impersonal manner" (1, 76 f.).

From all of this follows a conclusion of the greatest importance, namely, that everything we read in the Gospels really happened. The question of historicity need not be reopened with regard to particular texts. As Felder puts it (1, 116):

> When the authenticity and credibility of these historical books are once established, the apologist moves on firm ground. He has then the right unhesitatingly to draw his proofs from every part of the Gospels for the solution of all the problems which present themselves. He is, therefore, freed from the trouble of always examining anew the foundations, as he passes from question to question and from text to text. The Gospels are for him, in their full extent and in the strictest sense of the word, historical authorities and scientific evidence.

Assuming the historicity of the Gospels as proved, the apologist can now go about his proper task of demonstrating that Christ is a divine legate. This demonstration is accomplished in two stages, the first of which aims to show that Jesus really did claim to be Messiah and Son of God. The second stage then shows that He proved His claims by His prophecies, His miracles, and especially His resurrection. Some authors add a supplementary argument from the surpassing holiness of Jesus, which is shown to be a moral miracle.

The general conclusion of the historicist apologetic is that the Christian religion, having been founded by the divine Messiah, merits our unquestioning assent. The faith of the Evangelists is triumphantly vindicated, and this without recourse to any evidence other than that offered by the

Evangelists themselves. The Evangelists as factual historians prove the reasonableness of their own religious convictions!

Before we discuss the vulnerable points in this argument, we should pause to admire its structure. It proceeds by strict logical steps. By disposing of the problem of historicity independently of any study of the content of the Gospels, it immeasurably simplifies the process of apologetics. Moreover, in the properly apologetic section, it is satisfied with considering the words and actions of Jesus under the cold light of historical science. No appeal is made to the subjective concerns of the religious inquirer. An apologetics which could thus array itself in the garb of objective scientific history could not fail to impress an age which had unlimited esteem for the powers of positive historical method.

Nevertheless, even in the Victorian era, religious thinkers of real stature were ill at ease with the historicist apologetic. Writers such as Kierkegaard and Newman protested that history, considered as a purely scientific discipline, could not impose a definite religious interpretation of the person of Jesus. In this present generation many critics have pointed out the deficiencies of the historicist apologetic. The most powerful critique is perhaps that given by Jean Levie, S.J., in the first chapter of his *Sous les yeux de l'incroyant*.

Two main grievances are laid at the door of this apologetic. First, it misunderstands the limitations of history; second, it misconstrues the nature of the biblical sources. I shall here say something about the first of these charges, leaving the question of the nature of the Bible for the following chapter.

Academic history, as is clear, cannot be the final judge of truth and falsehood in matters of religion. It does not pretend to be able to pronounce on matters of philosophical

[11]

truth, aesthetic, ethical, or religious values. The object of technical history is simply the phenomenal past—past events, that is, as they appeared in their spatiotemporal relationships. The ultimate interpretation of the source and significance of such events cannot be achieved by historical research alone.

Even to say that the phenomenal past can be recovered by history is to risk exaggeration. Many historiographers maintain that the goal of their science is not to find out what really happened but rather to frame the most plausible hypothesis. The historian scrutinizes the documents and traces of past human activity and concocts a theory as to what may or must have transpired. The object of history, in this view, is not so much truth as verisimilitude. The historian as such seeks a hypothesis which economically accounts for the appearances. He is not absolutely committed to his own theory. As a good scientist he is always ready to readjust it to accommodate any new data which may come to light.

In determining what is likely to have occurred, the historian relies on postulates. He assumes that certain things are possible, others impossible; that men in certain situations react in certain ways. These postulates are in part a matter of common sense. To some extent, too, they depend on philosophical or theological preconceptions. Many would hold that the scientific historian must assume, at least as a working hypothesis, that all worldly events can be explained in terms of natural causes and conditions; he cannot, as a historian, appeal to the supernatural. At most he could say that a given event seems to be inexplicable in terms of the normal laws of history. To assign a transcendent cause would lie beyond the competence of academic history.

All this being granted, we may consider the limits of

what pure history could do with regard to establishing who Christ really was.

As regards the character and doctrine of Jesus, which would seem to lie within the province of historical inquiry, scientific history has failed to yield any agreed picture. There are as many different views as there are schools of historians. The differences in the results come neither from the materials studied (all rely upon the four Gospels as their main source) nor from their procedural method (which is positive historical inquiry). The disagreements arise principally from the different presuppositions with which historians address themselves to the problem. In deciding what has or lacks verisimilitude, postulates are all-important. If one approaches the New Testament materials with the previous judgment that religion is a matter of emotional experience, one will easily find in Jesus a master of the "religion of the heart." Another, approaching the same texts with the idea that religion essentially consists in ethical conduct, will readily conclude that Jesus was first and foremost a moral teacher. Some will find evident proofs that Jesus worked miracles; others will judge that the miracle stories are unreliable. The evidence can be lined up in a hundred different ways according to the perspectives of the inquirer. History alone is therefore powerless to impose any definite conclusions regarding the doctrine and behavior of Jesus.

Let us assume, however, that historical method could establish with overwhelming verisimilitude a definite picture concerning what Jesus had said and done. Would it follow then that history could tell us whether He was really the Messiah and the Son of God? A moment's reflection will suffice to answer in the negative. At its ideal best, scientific history, conducted according to the norms of the historico-critical school, can put us in the same situation as the original spectators. We have no reason to think that Jesus' contemporaries and associates found it easy to believe. Their faith did not issue more or less automatically from what they saw and heard. In his *Christianity and History* (pp. 125 f.) Prof. H. Butterfield has expressed this point very effectively:

If we remember as a solemn fact that those who saw Christ and heard Him were still divided in opinion about Him, we might doubt whether anything in the written Gospels or anything that historical science may discover will overcome such obstructions as exist or obliterate those factors which made possible so great a difference of opinion amongst those who saw the historical Jesus in the flesh. . . . If instead of the present narratives we had an undoubted autobiography of Christ; if He instead of St. Paul had left us great Epistles of unchallenged authenticity; if we had state documents concerning the public events of His life, I am not clear that the differences of judgment to-day would be a whit less sharp than they are, or the distribution of opinion very different. For the truth is that the essential question is not one of scholarship at all.

The apparent simplicity of the historicist apologetic thus turns out upon examination to be an illusion. Pure historical method, conceived according to the norms of the historico-critical school, is not fully competent to reconstruct the life and doctrine of Jesus on the phenomenal plane: it cannot by itself establish any solid and indisputable version of the words and works of the real Jesus. Still less is scientific history capable of settling the question of religious interpretation. Such interpretation lies within the competence of a man committed, or at least open, to religious values. A realistic apologetics therefore—one which aims to grapple with the genuine issues—cannot concentrate solely or even primarily on historical research. We have seen how this conclusion results from the very nature of academic history. The same conclusion will become even clearer in our next chapter, in which we shall assess the Gospels as scientific historical sources.

RECOMMENDED READINGS

HISTORICAL METHOD

L. Gottschalk, *Understanding History*. New York: Knopf, 1950. A well-balanced introduction by a professor from the University of Chicago.

H.-I. Marrou, "From the Logic of History to an Ethic for the Historian," *Cross Currents* 11, 1 (Winter, 1961), 61–77. An able critique of positivistic historiography by a distinguished Catholic historian.

THE HISTORIANS AND THE PROBLEM OF JESUS

G. Ricciotti, *The Life of Christ*. Milwaukee: Bruce, 1947. Pp. 179–216 give a convenient Catholic survey covering much the same ground as A. Schweitzer's brilliant but provocative *Quest of the Historical Jesus*.

CATHOLIC HISTORICIST APOLOGETICS

H. Felder, O.M.Cap., *Christ and the Critics*. 2 vols.; London: Burns Oates and Washbourne, 1924. A monumental attempt to turn the weapons of scientific historiography against the skeptical critics; first published in German in 1911.

LIMITS OF ACADEMIC HISTORY IN APOLOGETICS

H. Butterfield, *Christianity and History*. New York: Scribner's, 1950; reprinted paperback, 1961. A distinguished Protestant history professor from Cambridge University maintains that academic history can neither prove nor disprove the truth of Christianity.

J. Levie, S.J., *Sous les yeux de l'incroyant*. 2nd ed.; Brussels: Desclée de Brouwer, 1946. A collection of brilliant essays on apologetical themes by a noted Catholic exegete.

★ 2 ★

The Gospels and Scientific History

We have already considered one difficulty against what I have called the historicist apologetic, namely, that it over-estimates the capacity of technical history. After the academic historian has done his task, the student still finds himself faced by the same query that Jesus addressed to His contemporaries: "What do you think of the Christ? Whose son is He?" (Mt 22:42).

Let us now carry our critique one stage further by focusing on the Gospel materials. Are they such that pure history can hope to establish, with high verisimilitude, the precise nature of Jesus' claims or of the wonders by which He is alleged to have confirmed them? The importance of this question from the standpoint of the historicist apologetic needs no emphasis.

A generation or two ago, the defenders of orthodoxy were accustomed to rest their case on two arguments: first, the Gospels were held to embody eyewitness reports; second, these reports were affirmed to be strictly factual. How well do these two arguments stand up in the light of contemporary biblical scholarship?

The problem of authorship is, of course, far too complicated to deal with in a few pages. I can only hope to give some very general indications regarding the current trends. In the past, Catholic apologists insisted quite vehemently on the strict authenticity of the four Gospels, which meant that two of them, Matthew and John, would have been the actual writings of companions of our Lord, and that the other two would come from close associates of apostles.

Today Catholic scholars write in much more modest terms. As regards the first Gospel, we have some valuable indications by early ecclesiastical writers—Papias in particular—that the apostle Matthew wrote down the "sayings (*logia*) of the Lord" in a Hebrew idiom (which is generally taken to mean in Aramaic). But the links between this hypothetical Semitic document and the first canonical Gospel are tenuous and obscure. A leading Catholic authority, Alfred Wikenhauser, writes in his *New Testament Introduction* (p. 195):

> It may be taken as certain that an Aramaic original of the Gospel of St. Matthew can be defended only if we regard Greek Mt. not as a literal translation of the Aramaic, but as a thorough revision made with frequent use of the Gospel of St. Mark. . . . Since there are no remains of Aramaic Matthew, and no one knows what it was like, we cannot make any more accurate or more definite statement about the relationship between the two forms of St. Matthew's Gospel.

Any number of contemporary Catholic biblical scholars could be quoted in the same sense. It is quite widely held that the Gospel of Matthew, in the form in which we have it, is the latest of the Synoptics, that it shows considerable dependence on Mark and represents a further development of much of the Marcan material. It also includes non-Marcan materials, some of which might derive from the apostle Matthew. But scientific source criticism does not permit us to affirm with confidence that any particular phrase or sentence in the first canonical Gospel is vouched for by the apostle himself.

[18]

With regard to the fourth Gospel, the historical evidences in favor of its ascription to the apostle John are far from apodictic. Most non-Catholic scholars attribute it either to a certain "John the Presbyter" or to an unknown disciple of the apostle who lived at Ephesus. Catholic scholarship continues to insist that the fourth Gospel comes from the apostle John in the sense that it embodies his memories and reflections; but many are willing to admit (as does Fr. Raymond E. Brown in the recent *New Testament Reading Guide*) that the actual redaction was the work of an unknown disciple-editor. Since the question is so vexed, the contemporary biblical scholar will be very hesitant to affirm that any given statement in the fourth Gospel is surely guaranteed to us by the apostle himself.

As for St. Luke, his association with the apostle Paul is generally admitted. But that association does not greatly enhance his authority as an Evangelist, since Paul himself never knew our Lord in the flesh. In his prologue Luke tells us that he used a variety of sources. He consulted eyewitnesses and preachers of the word; he also made use of the written accounts which were already in circulation—including almost certainly the Gospel of Mark. Because of the variety of the sources used, it is hard to say with regard to any individual sentence in Luke that it rests upon the testimony of immediate eyewitnesses.

The second Gospel is probably the most primitive of the four. It is commonly admitted to have been written at Rome by a companion of Peter named Mark. He is probably the same person as the John Mark mentioned in Acts and in other New Testament writings. While not an immediate witness of Jesus' life, Mark no doubt made extensive use of what he had heard in Peter's preaching. Careful analysis of the text, however, reveals that he had other sources as well. The identification of those sections which are most likely to rest on Peter's preaching is a matter of conjecture. Vincent Taylor, in his celebrated edition of Mark, has made a rather plausible distribution of matter into "Petrine" and "non-Petrine." He considers that about one third of the second Gospel shows signs of direct dependence on the reminiscences of an eyewitness, probably Peter. (Out of 661 verses for the entire Gospel, some 150 verses of the public life and, more conjecturally, some 70 verses of the Passion narrative are designated "Petrine.")

In conclusion, therefore, we can find many bonds which connect the Gospels with immediate witnesses. But we can hardly go along with the contention of Fillion, already referred to, that the four Gospels are for all practical purposes eyewitness accounts.

In connection with the authorship of the Gospels, it may be helpful to add a few remarks concerning their dates. In general, Protestant critics have rejected the extreme views that were sometimes propounded in the mid-nineteenth century, when D. F. Strauss and F. C. Baur, among others, declared that all the Gospels, except possibly Matthew, were written after 150. Today there is rather close agreement among the leading scholars of the various confessions. A representative Protestant, Vincent Taylor, in his *The Gospels: A Short Introduction* (9th ed.; London: Epworth Press, 1960), conjectures that Mark, the earliest Gospel, was written about 65–70, Luke about 80–85, Matthew about 85–90, and John about 90–100. Most Catholic scholars would find these dates acceptable, give or take five years, in the cases of Mark and John. For Matthew, the majority of Catholics would prefer a date before 70, but a few say after 70 (Wikenhauser) and perhaps about 80 (Stanley). For Luke, Catholic critics incline toward a date between 64 and 70, but Wikenhauser considers it later than 70, perhaps no sooner than 80. For our present purposes, there is no need to choose between these opinions; it will suffice to take note of them. So far as apologetics is concerned, the strongest arguments are those which do not depend on the prior acceptance of a very early date for the Gospels. Thus, it is generally advisable not to place too much reliance on arguments which would be invalid if, say, Luke or Matthew were written after 70 A.D.

The dates in the preceding paragraph have reference to the Gospels as wholes. They apply to the Gospels as we read them today, with all their parts, except for a few short passages which are considered to be additions to the original Gospels. In chapter 4 we shall be concerned with two such passages: the canonical ending of Mark (16: 9–20) and the twenty-first chapter of John. While these sections are, according to all Catholics, canonical and inspired, they were probably not part of the Gospels as first composed. Many critics hold that they were written by early editors, perhaps close associates of the Evangelists. However that may be, it is at least difficult to demonstrate that they are the work of the Evangelists themselves. For purposes of apologetics, it is better to prescind from their authorship.

So much for the questions of authorship and date. Our next question, equally crucial for the historicist apologetic, has to do with the so-called veracity of the Gospels. A simplistic solution would be to say that the Evangelists either intended to report actual facts or they were liars. Nobody today holds that they were liars. But there is great diversity of opinion in assessing the degree and kind of historical truth in the Gospels. The basic issue has to do with the so-called "literary genre." The Gospels do not profess to be memoirs or even, in the modern sense, biographies. They are, first and foremost, "gospels," that is to say, proclamations of the good news of what God has done for mankind in Jesus Christ. The Gospels are not the work of detached observers, whose first aim is descriptive accuracy. They are written *ex fide* (as expressions of faith) and *in fidem* (to kindle faith in the reader).

The literary genre of the Gospels obviously raises some very acute questions as to their value as historical sources. Since the Evangelists wrote as fervent believers in the risen Lord, it may well be asked if they were still in a position to report with detailed accuracy on how the words and actions of Christ would have appeared in His own lifetime, before the events of Easter. And since they wrote as servants of the word, in furtherance of the Church's aims, we must frankly face the question whether they felt themselves obliged to give a strictly factual report on the occurrences of our Lord's earthly life. How can we be sure that the narrative has not been colored to a greater or lesser degree by doctrinal, apologetical, and liturgical considerations? This is not simply a captious objection raised by the enemies of Christian revelation, but a genuine problem in the minds of many sincere believers, including Catholics.

In addressing ourselves to this question, we should not simply proceed a priori. We must take what Fr. Vincent O'Keefe has called "a good, long, serious look" at the Gospels themselves, checking their similarities and differences. In the case of the first three Gospels, the similarities are such that we can detect signs of mutual dependence and use of common sources. For the Johannine Gospel, the differences are so great as to make it evident that its author relied primarily on other traditions.

A comparative study of the first three Gospels throws much light on the extent to which the authors considered themselves free to alter what they found in their sources. Catholic critics, as well as Protestants, have done fruitful work in this field in the past few decades. In the bibliographical note at the end of this chapter, reference is made to several recent articles.

In studying the Gospel of Matthew, it is most helpful to keep one's eye on the parallel passages in the other Synoptics. Rather frequently he introduces professions of faith which are lacking in the other accounts. Thus, after the incident of Christ's walking on the water, Matthew adds: "They who were in the boat came and worshiped Him, saying, 'Truly thou art the Son of God'" (14:33). This is quite different from Mark's account, which concludes with the observation that the disciples were confused, because their hearts were still blinded (6:51 f.). It would be artificial to try to harmonize these remarks, as though both were strictly factual. Similarly, the differences between Matthew's narrative of the confession of Peter at Caesarea Philippi (Mt 16:16–20) and the parallel accounts in the other Synoptics have prompted many critics, both Catholic and non-Catholic, to remark that Matthew is evidently exercising a certain liberty in rearranging or amplifying the materials which he finds in his sources.

Luke, too, feels authorized to modify his materials. Especially is this true in matters of chronology. In accordance with his announced purpose of writing an orderly account (1:3), he frequently rearranges the sequence of events so as to bring out their significance more clearly. For example, he places our Lord's rejection at Nazareth at the opening of the public life rather than near the end of His Galilean ministry, as in Mark and Matthew. He likewise transposes the order of the three temptations of Christ, in order to make it fit better into the general plan of his Gospel.

Many critics have found signs in both Matthew and Luke that certain sayings of our Lord about the coming destruction of Jerusalem were made more concrete in the light of the events which, at the time of the redaction of the Gospels, had already come to pass. This is obviously a delicate question, but I cannot avoid mentioning it to show some of the problems which the apologist must deal with if he wants to argue from the words which the Evangelists place on the lips of Christ.

It would be possible to give an almost endless list of discrepancies among the three Synoptic Gospels in reporting the same events. One could cite, for instance, the different versions of the Our Father, which has seven petitions in Matthew and five in Luke, or of the Beatitudes, where Luke has only four of the eight or nine in Matthew. Even the miracles of our Lord are quite differently reported in various Gospels. Divergences of this nature, as Fr. O'Keefe has said, "serve to counteract any naive understanding of the Gospels as some sort of photographic representation of the life of Christ. . . . The Gospels have a freedom in the order of the facts, in their presentation, in the very redaction of the words of Christ, which shows that their authors did not feel bound to the repetition of a definitive formula" (*Catholic Biblical Quarterly* 21 [1959], 173 f.).

Matthew and Luke do not, to be sure, radically innovate. We never find them inventing, so to speak, out of whole cloth. But those minor changes which they do introduce should make us cautious in assuming that in any given instance we know exactly what we should have seen or heard if we had been on the spot. What is here said of the Synoptics applies a fortiori to John, whose testimony is not greatly esteemed by positivistic historians.

The Liberal critics of the nineteenth century, while they placed little faith in Matthew and Luke, and dismissed John as pure allegory, often maintained that Mark, as the earliest Evangelist, had composed a historically reliable account, practically free from theological interpretation. But since the studies of Wrede and K. L. Schmidt this view has become quite untenable. Mark is no more interested in writing an impartial historical document than the other Evangelists. In his first sentence he announces his intention of heralding "the gospel of Jesus Christ, the Son of God." On every page he exhibits and appeals for faith in Jesus. His entire narrative leads swiftly from incident to incident toward its climax, when the centurion on Calvary exclaims: "Truly this man was the Son of God." This expression is obviously something more than a historical recollection. It differs markedly from the parallel passage in Luke, who has the centurion declare: "Truly this was a just man."

So far we have spoken of how the Evangelists modified the materials that came to them in the tradition. The next question relates to the fidelity of the tradition itself. What happened to the story of Jesus as it was told and retold by preachers and catechists in the generation between the crucifixion and the editing of the first Gospel? Was the oral tradition during these years handed down in fixed formulas or was it in a state of flux? The early form critics in the 1920's gave a very radical answer to this question. They attributed practically everything to the creative faith of the community.

[25]

The champions of orthodoxy often reacted by going to the opposite extreme. Some tried to account for the Gospel tradition as a whole by supposing that the smallest details of our Lord's life, and the very words which He had uttered, were memorized and repeated in Talmudic fashion. Contemporary criticism is seeking to find some sort of *via media*. Most biblical scholars would now hold that the tradition was faithful without being servile; it transmitted the words and deeds of Jesus with such adaptations as were required to render them intelligible and significant for a different generation living in a different environment. The Church, possessing the Holy Spirit, felt authorized to exercise a holy liberty. If this seems scandalous to the modern critical historian, he should remind himself that the accepted notions of history in our time are the product of a scientific age and had no place in the ancient Mediterranean world—a point stressed by Pius XII in the Encyclical *Divino afflante Spiritu*.

The question, therefore, how much factual historicity is to be found in the New Testament record calls for a very complex answer. It is a gross oversimplification to content oneself with saying, as some of the older apologists did, that the Gospels are historical. Undoubtedly they are historical, but what kind of historicity do we have? Do we have the kind of history that permits us to reconstruct in detail what a neutral spectator would have seen and heard on this or that occasion? This question cannot be answered in general.

The Gospels, as we have seen, are composed out of many blocks of different materials, each having its own provenance and literary type. Each section of material must be studied for its own sake in order to determine its particular kind and degree of historicity. We do not have the same historicity in the Infancy Gospels as in the Passion narratives. The fresh, informal Marcan narratives do not have exactly the same quality of history as one finds in the highly stylized, reflective accounts in the fourth Gospel. With reference to the sayings and sermons of Jesus, Fr. David Stanley, writing in *Theological Studies* in 1959 (pp. 585 f.), has observed:

> With regard to sayings and sermons of Jesus, there are some logia which undoubtedly retain the form and idiom of the speaker. But there are also discourses which the Evangelist himself has constructed from Jesus' sayings and sermons; and these can even be expressed (as in the fourth Gospel) in the author's own style and terminology. There are parables which in the course of oral tradition have undergone a certain historicization or allegorization. At times we find liturgical texts which enshrine pronouncements of Jesus dealing with the ritual or sacramental life of His future Church.

The task of historical criticism is not a proper field for amateurs. It is a highly technical work, making demands on all the skills which go into the formation of a biblical scholar. Before venturing a responsible opinion as to the historicity of a given text, one must consider all that archeology, philology, textual criticism, and comparative religion can contribute to illuminate the point. In most matters we must be content with a provisional and probable answer. Certitude is a rare and precious jewel.

Thanks to the painstaking researches of biblical scholars of all faiths, much progress has been made in the past few decades. Responsible opinion is far less divided today than it was a generation or two ago. Nobody holds any longer that the Christ of faith has totally eclipsed the Jesus of history, or that Jesus is a mere myth. As Fr. Léon-Dufour has said, "There is unquestionably an objective historical substratum which imposes itself regardless of one's beliefs or sympathy for the Christian phenomenon" (*Introduction à la Bible* 2, 332 f.). All reputable scholars would agree that Jesus was a religious teacher who lived in Palestine and who sought to purify and reform the worship of Judaism. He was followed by a group of intimate disciples, mostly from Galilee. The crowds looked upon Him as a wonder-worker and even hailed Him as the promised Messiah. His increasing influence aroused bitter opposition from the priests and Pharisees, and led to His trial and crucifixion under Pontius Pilate.

But those elements of the life of Jesus which, in the view of independent scholarship, are recoverable by sheerly historical techniques are not of much help for apologetics. The apologist's real problem begins just where the consensus leaves off. His concern is to establish that Jesus not only had a reputation for prodigies but that He really performed them; that He was not only looked upon as Messiah but that He understood Himself to be both Messiah and God; that He not only died on a cross but left the tomb and appeared again to His disciples.

On points such as these one still finds a rather sharp division of opinion. Believers in the Christ of dogma, whether Protestant or Catholic, generally feel that the historical evidence decisively points toward the conclusion that Jesus did claim a transcendent and Messianic dignity, that He did work remarkable prodigies, that the tomb was actually empty on Easter Sunday, etc. In support of this view one can call attention to the convergence of all the traditions which have left their traces on the New Testament. On historical grounds the most economical hypothesis would seem to be that Jesus spoke and acted substantially as the Gospels recount.

A historian who denies the Incarnation, however, will vigorously dissent. He will say that as a scientific man he is obliged to proceed on the postulate that things have natural explanations. In his eyes miracles are so unlikely that their possibility need not be taken seriously. Just as the Catholic refuses to admit that Apollonius of Tyana raised the dead, so the non-Christian historian is unmoved by the miracle stories in the Gospel. Since he denies the reality of Christ's miracles, he will have to hold that the Gospels are unhistorical when they relate such things as the calming of tempests, the multiplication of loaves, the curing of lepers, and the raising of the dead. If all of this is legend, one must necessarily conclude that the Gospels are rather unreliable as historical sources.

This quarrel about the historical value of the Gospels obviously cannot be settled by the techniques of history itself. As we saw in chapter 1, the historian as such cannot justify his own postulates nor can he pass judgment on the religious personality of Jesus. So far as pure history is concerned, therefore, the conflict between the believer and the unbeliever is irreducible. To overcome the opposition, we must transfer the debate to some other ground.

Must we at this point engage our believing opponent in an abstract philosophical discussion about the antecedent possibility of miracles? Or can we usefully make some further appeal to the New Testament? Do the Gospels themselves tend to show that the believer holds the more reasonable position? Personally, I am convinced that they do. I firmly hold that they furnish persuasive arguments not only for the real existence of the man Jesus but for His miracles, His resurrection, His Messiahship, and His divinity. But in order to perceive the force of these arguments, it is necessary to contemplate the Gospels in far wider perspectives than those of technical history. We must consider them not simply as historical documents but as religious testimonies addressed to us by the primitive Church.

RECOMMENDED READINGS

AUTHORSHIP OF THE GOSPELS

A. Wikenhauser, *New Testament Introduction*. New York: Herder and Herder, 1958.

New Testament Reading Guide. Collegeville, Minn.: Liturgical Press, 1960–62. A series of fourteen pamphlets dealing with the New Testament in general and each New Testament book in particular.

HISTORICITY OF THE GOSPELS

X. Léon-Dufour, S.J., "Les évangiles et l'histoire," in A. Robert and A. Feuillet (ed.), *Introduction à la Bible* 2 (Paris: Desclée, 1959), 322–34.

F. J. McCool, S.J., "The Preacher and the Historical Witness of the Gospels," *Theological Studies* 21 (1960), 517–43. Cf. *Theology Digest* 9, 3 (Autumn, 1961), 145–47.

V. O'Keefe, S.J., "Towards Understanding the Gospels," *Catholic Biblical Quarterly* 21 (1959), 171–89. Cf. *Theology Digest* 9, 1 (Winter, 1961), 9–13.

D. M. Stanley, S.J., "The Conception of Our Gospels as Salvation-History," *Theological Studies* 20 (1959), 561–89. Cf. *Theology Digest* 9, 1 (Winter, 1961), 23–25.

N.B. Several articles on the historicity of the Gospels, including those by Fr. O'Keefe and Fr. Stanley listed above, are reproduced in the anthology *Faith, Reason, and the Gospels,* edited by John J. Heaney, S.J., published by The Newman Press, 1961.

* 3 *

The Gospels as Confessional
Documents

Measured by the standards of von Ranke or Bernheim, our four Gospels, as we have seen, are far from ideal historical sources. They are not easily traceable to eyewitnesses. The authors, moreover, make no pretense to impartiality; they write frankly as worshiping believers. The diversities between John and the Synoptics, and among Synoptics themselves, make it clear that the Evangelists do not aim at photographic accuracy. The pure historian, therefore, will treat the Gospels with great caution. He will not deny that Jesus existed or was an influential religious teacher, but he will be suspicious of precisely those details to which the Christian apologist will wish to appeal, namely, the divine claims and miracles of Jesus. On these matters the profane historian will not find the testimony of the Gospels sufficiently primitive and unbiased to upset his own postulates. He will adhere to his presumption that worldly events have natural explanations, and will expunge the supernatural elements from the life of Jesus as best he can.

At this point the Christian historicist will experience a sense of distress. He will regret the way in which the Evangelists went about their task. A little impatiently, he will ask why they did not identify themselves and their sources more accurately. Why did they not reproduce more exactly what they found in their fonts rather than tamper with it as we have seen? Why did they not obtain and pass on to us more precise details about the words and miracles of our Lord? From this point of view it seems regrettable that we have only the testimony of believers. Would not the Evangelists have done better to incorporate some depositions from neutral witnesses, such as medical reports of the type that the modern Church demands for canonization processes?

Felder and his school would convert all adversaries by summoning them before the bar of academic history. But the summons would be in vain. The case cannot be proved by the rules of historical evidence. Much of what the Evangelists have to say would be simply ruled out of court.

So far as positivistic history is concerned, we are therefore at an impasse. If the deadlock is to be broken, appeal must be made to a different type of argument. One approach might be to base one's apologetic exclusively on the properties of the Catholic Church as she exists in the modern world. But I think it would be a mistake to abandon the New Testament so early. We must not undersell the persuasive power of the Gospels, which has been experienced by countless souls over the ages. Innumerable inquirers have felt their doubts dissolve and their convictions solidify as they have read the story of Jesus in the Bible. This fact is of vital moment for apologetics. If we could only penetrate the secret power of the Gospels to kindle and intensify the flame of faith, we should be in a far better position to construct a valid apologetic theory.

To some extent we are here in the field of mystery. We shall never fully understand the dynamic efficacy of the biblical word, "more piercing than a two-edged sword"

(Heb 4:12). The inspired expressions of Scripture possess an unction that is lacking to ordinary human speech. According to St. Thomas, God gives a special charism to the ministers of His word—the "grace of speech"—thanks to which they can communicate their faith to others (*Summa theol.* 2–2, q. 177, a. 1, ad 4m). This same gift was undoubtedly accorded, in a very high degree, to the biblical authors. For this reason one can agree with Cardinal Bea that "the very words of Holy Scripture, read and explained with the necessary dispositions, possess an inherent light and force that surpass the light and force of human words, and give them singular and unique authority and power" (*Maison-Dieu,* 1956, p. 138). The Bible has a quasi-sacramental efficacy. When a man reads the Gospels reverently and prayerfully, the Holy Spirit will certainly be at work in his heart, inwardly inclining him to assent to the truth. The Calvinists have made much—even too much—of the "inward witness of the Holy Spirit"; but long centuries before Calvin it was already Catholic doctrine that it is the Holy Spirit "who gives sweetness and joy to all in accepting the truth in faith" (Council of Arles, *DB* 180; cf. Vatican Council I, *DB* 1791).

The convincing power of the New Testament, then, may be chiefly attributed to the inspiring grace of God. Nevertheless, grace builds on nature. The Christian message, to be acceptable, must possess a certain natural credibility. Therefore it is legitimate to ask how the proclamation of the Gospel, as we encounter it in the New Testament, commends itself to human reason. Apologetics must occupy itself with this problem.

We shall utterly fail to answer this question unless we note at the beginning that the New Testament is throughout its length and breadth an urgent call for faith. There is nothing scientific or academic in the Gospels. They aim to transmit not a photograph of Jesus as He might have appeared to a detached observer, but a portrait of Jesus as understood by the believing Church. This numinous portrait is not simply a thing to be admired from afar. It is an appeal to faith and adoration. The reader is on every page invited to join the Church in her devout confession.

This frankly confessional aspect of the Gospels has as one result that it is unnatural to read them with critical detachment. Jesus Himself, as He lives in the pages of the New Testament, addresses Himself to men. As I read of Him conversing with Peter or Pilate, Mary or John, I become conscious that He is also speaking to me, demanding from me the unqualified surrender of faith. This is not a mere piece of dramatic artifice, but a dreadfully serious challenge. The Evangelists themselves, and the Church through them, solemnly guarantee the reality of Christ's call. The Gospels, therefore, confront the reader with an existential choice. Either I must accept Jesus, with His sovereign demands upon me, or I must refuse what He asks. To look upon Him with mere interest, to remain deliberately uncommitted, is in effect to reject Him. "He who does not believe shall be condemned" (Mk 16:16).

As confessional documents, the Gospels speak only to potential or actual believers. They contain nothing to satisfy the imagination of the novelist or the curiosity of the chronicler. They do not present Jesus "according to the flesh" but as seen in the light of the Spirit. Only to the man who is earnestly seeking communion with God will the Gospels yield their full message.

This suggests a possible way out of the stalemate to which

[34]

we have alluded. On the plane of academic history there is no escape from the deadlock between the believer and the infidel. But suppose we follow the bidding of the Gospels themselves and move to the terrain of religious concern. Here we may hope for a solution. The religious inquirer, since he does not have the same objectives as the profane historian, will have to adopt different postulates and methods.

Academic history, as we have noted, is primarily directed toward recovering the past in its observable aspects. It does not deal with imponderables except secondarily and indirectly. The religious man, however, will not be intent upon externals. He will be concerned with discovering the religious significance of the past events.

What method can possibly enable us to penetrate beneath the veil of outer appearances into the very sanctuary of Jesus' inner life? This is not a matter of common observation. There are depths in any man's existence which he reveals only to his friends. A friend alone has the affective kinship required to assimilate such knowledge. If I wish to know the heart and soul of another, and to get beyond superficial conjectures, I must either become his intimate companion or rely on the personal testimony of those who have known him familiarly.

Jesus, according to the Gospels, did reveal Himself to a band of privileged followers. He selected them carefully and prepared them by long training to receive this personal communication. To them he disclosed His relationship to the eternal Father and the mysteries of His divine life. "I have called you friends, because all things that I have heard from my Father I have made known to you. You have not chosen me, but I have chosen you" (Jn 15:15 f.). Jesus designated them as the witnesses and heralds of these mysteries. "You are to bear witness, because from the beginning you are with me" (Jn 15:27).

Once we have grasped the spiritual nature of their mission, we can easily see why the apostles and Evangelists write as they do. It would be utterly inappropriate for them to offer documentary proofs and to hold themselves to the rules of judicial evidence. They can afford to be frankly partisan and to be careless of points of chronology, geography, and descriptive detail. All this in no way detracts from their religious testimony. As witnesses to the mind and spirit of Jesus, which animated all His actions, they are unsurpassable. Their loyal enthusiasm, far from making them untrustworthy, only renders their witness the more impressive. It manifests the power of Jesus to captivate men's hearts. We can, of course, reject the New Testament interpretation of Jesus, but we cannot manufacture a substitute. The inner secrets of our Lord's soul must be accepted on the authority of His intimate friends, as guaranteed by the sacred tradition, or else be lost forever.

But how can we be sure that the picture of Jesus proposed to us in the New Testament is not a mere projection of some human religious ideal? We have seen the difficulty of resolving this question by the techniques of academic history, which would seek to show that it is the sole interpretation of which the recoverable facts about Jesus will admit. A more fruitful approach, in my opinion, consists in a study of the qualities of the testimony itself.

In matters of personal attestation we have no ready-made criteriology. The norms of reliability have never been set forth so precisely as those for factual reporting. Perhaps they do not admit of abstract analysis. However this may be, there are, I suggest, excellent reasons for judging that the evangelical portrait of Jesus is credible. The concrete logic by which we arrive at this conclusion can be described in terms of various indices.

In the first place, the New Testament unquestionably reflects the way in which Jesus was understood by the band of His immediate disciples. There may be variations in the way in which individual incidents are narrated or in the precise language attributed to Jesus on this or that occasion. But the whole biblical testimony converges to give us a single vision of Christ. There are many theologies in the New Testament but only one faith. This overriding unity evidently implies that the traditions were kept free from the contamination of rumor. They were not fabricated at will by an anonymous community. On the contrary, the Gospel testimonies were composed and collected within the Church under the vigilance of the apostles and their successors. Recent studies of the processes of transmission employed in rabbinic and early Christian circles—such as those of H. Riesenfeld and B. Gerhardsson—tend to show that the words and deeds of Jesus must have been handed down as a holy deposit by well-schooled and tested "servants of the word." The New Testament is, therefore, a reliable record of the impression made by Jesus on His original companions, and of the growing insight of the Church into her initial faith.

Secondly, the New Testament faith about Jesus is proclaimed with the stoutest conviction. In reading the New Testament one cannot fail to be struck by the absolute firmness of its religious witness. The authors never write like philosophers groping for the final answer, nor does the language of doubt ever appear in their religious testimony. They transmit their message as something that has been manifested to them with blinding clarity.

Thirdly, the New Testament doctrine about Christ is utterly novel. Nothing in the Jewish tradition—the tradition in which Peter and Andrew, James and John, Stephen and Paul and Barnabas were reared—would have predisposed them to accept what they now proclaim. Before they became Christians they would have shrunk in horror at the very thought of paying divine honors to a man. How can one explain, if not through a revelation, that they now so confidently and unanimously look upon this Galilean carpenter as Lord of the universe?

Fourthly, there is the fact that the apostles themselves were transformed into new men by the tidings which they bore. We sense this not only from the story of their deeds but from the very style in which they and their companions write. In becoming Christians they have received the power to set the universe on fire with the contagion of their vision, their hope, their unextinguishable love. The word lodged in their minds has become a dynamic force compelling them to go forth and preach to all mankind. Nothing in the formation of most of them—whether as fishermen, tax collectors, or tentmakers—would have made them likely candidates for such a mission.

Fifthly, one must consider the intrinsic qualities of the Christian message. It is not the type of message which is easily fabricated by the ingenuity of the wise, let alone by the wanderings of disordered minds. Two thousand years ago it was capable of regenerating an exhausted and disillusioned world. And still today each reader of the Gospels, if he have the least spark of religious concern, feels that it could do the same for him. Its tidings are powerful to deliver man from the aimlessness, selfishness, and pettiness of ordinary existence, to purify the heart and evoke the highest energies of the spirit. Who is there that can deny that he would be a better man if he believed more fervently in Christ or a worse one if he renounced his faith?

The heart of this message, the greatest marvel of all, is the portrait of Jesus which we find deeply imbedded in all the four Gospels. If men of the first century, whether Jews or Gentiles, had been asked to conjecture in what form God might appear on earth, none would have imagined Him coming in such a guise, so humble, gentle, and utterly human. Who would have dreamed of the divine Good Shepherd? In the Gospel portrait of Jesus there is nothing wooden or stereotyped. "His reactions are never conventional or foreseeable, they are always original and spirited" (H. Urs von Balthasar). He constantly does the most unexpected things, revolutionizing the accepted norms of conduct. He praises pagans and prostitutes, draws near to Samaritans and lepers. He attacks the most respected classes, and insults His hosts at dinner. In the midst of His intense labors He finds time to welcome little children to Himself. He rebukes the wind and the waves, but falls silent before His accusers. Men would never have fabricated such a figure as their religious leader, and precisely for this reason the Gospels have undying power to convert human hearts. After reading them we can only exclaim: this rings true. This spendthrift charity is properly divine. This is what God must really be, and if He were to become man, this is how He would behave.

The rational inquirer must seek to give some explanation for the genesis of the extraordinary faith and the unique religious society depicted for us in the New Testament. One answer is that given by the New Testament writers themselves. On every page they proclaim that they have not invented this doctrine, but that it has come to them through revelation. Jesus Himself has imparted the saving truth through His own words and works. If we accept that explanation, we can readily account for all the attributes we have just noted in the message and in the witness of the primitive Church. If it be false, the faith of the first Christians is an enigma.

In some such way as this it is possible, I think, to construct a New Testament apologetic which effectively supplies what is lacking to the historicist argument. The miracles of Jesus are not easily recoverable by sheerly historical techniques. But the testimony of the Apostolic Church, immortally enshrined in the New Testament, is in its way miraculous. A religion so lofty in content, so novel, so unanimous, so self-assured, so effortless, so joyful, so fruitful in good works, so durable in adversity—such a religion, I say, has all the marks of a divine revelation. And every other hypothesis proves on examination to be seriously deficient.

This apologetic of religious testimony, which takes its departure from the New Testament considered as a confessional document, has many advantages over the historicist polemic, which would look upon the New Testament as a mere record of fact. For one thing, it respects the intentions of the Evangelists themselves. They know nothing of the modern dichotomy between historical fact and religious interpretation. They present the reader with both together, asking for his assent to both on the same ground. To separate their factual reporting from their religious attestation is to perform a cruel vivisection which in the long run is fatal to both. The adventures of non-Catholic biblical criticism over

[40]

the past century make it evident that he who rejects the Christ of faith will soon end up by reducing the Jesus of history to a pale figure without religious significance. Conversely, he who makes light of the flesh-and-blood Jesus of history in the name of a more spiritual faith will end up prostrating himself before a timeless myth. If we are true to the Gospels, we shall insist on retaining both fact and interpretation, both history and faith. They are as inseparable as matter and form.

A second advantage of a confessional apologetic should also be noted. The much-vaunted objectivity of the historicist approach is apologetically sterile, for it diverts man's attention from precisely those valuational considerations on which his decision about Christ must ultimately turn. Scientific historical investigation tries to prescind as far as possible from questions of value, since these cannot be handled by the method. The academic historian must maintain an attitude of cold detachment. As a scientist, he constructs theories, but remains at every moment ready to abandon his current theory for a better one. He is intellectually and emotionally uncommitted. To pass directly from academic historical inquiry to an act of faith would be no easier than for a satellite to rise without a launching pad.

An apologetic such as we have outlined, which seeks to appraise the religious testimony of the Gospels, leads up far more smoothly to the personal surrender of faith. It forces the inquirer from the beginning to look upon Christianity as a religious message, and to face up to the religious challenge of the Gospels.

An apologetic which would take its departure from the proclamation of the primitive Church is, in the third place, very Catholic. It strikes at the roots of that false individualism which would seem to authorize a purely private approach to the religious problem. To accept Jesus without His disciples, in isolation from the circle of His followers, would be a monstrous thing, quite contrary to what He Himself, or any Israelite religious figure, would have intended. In the symposium *The Root of the Vine* (pp. 55 f.), the great Lutheran scholar Anton Fridrichsen has expressed this excellently:

> An Israelite prophet or a Jewish Messiah cannot be understood solely in terms of Western thought in the nineteenth century. The man of God is never isolated. He is always the centre of a circle taught by his words and example, in which his manner of life and teaching continues after his death. What is taught and written in this circle is ultimately derived from its founder and embodies his life and character. When we, the children of a later age and of another culture, wish to understand such a person and his period, we must return to tradition and inquire there; but our inquiry must be made with due understanding of local peculiarities. Only with such a sympathetic understanding is it possible to estimate a tradition as a source of history. No appreciation can be acquired without insight into the habits of life and thought of prophetic circles in ancient Israel, or of Jews of Rabbinic education and Messianic outlook. It will become clear that tradition is an excellent source of history, if the history we have in mind is the conduct of life in associations governed and influenced by persons who in some extraordinary way speak with divine authority. . . . No conception of [such a person] can be formed except by observing how he was remembered, described and quoted, and what was handed down about him. All these things form a totality of which he was the soul, because he did not keep his soul to himself, but gave himself to those who received his words, his nature and his will into themselves.

Once it is perceived that there can be no authentic portrait of Jesus except that based on the collective testimony of His disciples, we are on the road to a very Catholic view of

Christianity. It will easily be seen that an act of faith in Jesus inevitably involves a certain faith in human witnesses by whom He has chosen to perpetuate His memory on earth. In the last analysis, therefore, the logical alternatives are a faith which goes out to Christ and His Church together, or a thoroughgoing skepticism which refuses to accept either.

The New Testament is not simply a document about Christ. Not even the Gospels are this. They are documents about Christ as the Church sees and reacts to Him, or about the Church as it sees and reacts to Christ. It is this spectacle of Christ addressing His Church, and of the Church responding to Christ, which is the great sign of Christian credibility. A merely individualist view of Christ is an optical illusion; it is a mirage; it is not really a view of Christ at all.

Finally, we should recall that every apologetic should be adapted to the spirit of the age. The present generation is not likely to be moved by a historicist apologetic. Modern man has little confidence in the demonstrative powers of technical history, especially in the field of religious truth. He seeks an approach to God that is more properly personal. The personalist categories of testimony, invitation, response, engagement, fidelity, and communion—all of which have been so brilliantly opened up by contemporary existential philosophers—can and should be exploited in apologetics. We should not tie our defense of the faith to the corpse of a defunct historicism.

Such, then, are the general lines of an apologetic which builds on the Gospels as confessional documents rather than as sheerly objective historical sources. It remains for us to make this more concrete by concentrating on two problems that are crucial for Christian credibility: the resurrection and the divinity of Jesus.

RECOMMENDED READINGS

A. Fridrichsen, "Jesus, St. John, and St. Paul," in *The Root of the Vine: Essays in Biblical Theology*. New York: Philosophical Library, 1953, pp. 37–62. A Scandinavian Lutheran scholar points out the inapplicability of modern liberal critical norms to the religious traditions of the Near East in ancient times.

J. Guitton, *Jésus*. Paris: Grasset, 1956. Part 3, "Difficulté de croire au témoignage," gives some stimulating reflections on the structure of religious testimony and its place in apologetics.

G. Marcel, *The Philosophy of Existence*. London: Harvill Press, 1948. Chapter 3, "Testimony and Existentialism," is an excellent phenomenological analysis of what it means to be a witness.

J. H. Newman, *An Essay in Aid of a Grammar of Assent*. A profound investigation of the sources of religious conviction. Section 10 gives some applications in the field of Christian apologetics.

* 4 *

The Resurrection: History and Confession

We have contrasted two forms of apologetics, both based on the New Testament. The first of these would proceed by scientific historical techniques according to the postulates of the historicocritical school. The other would take a larger and more human view of the biblical testimony, attending expressly to questions of value. The first approach would seek to get behind the faith of the primitive Church and to prove its reasonability from the historically ascertainable facts related in the Gospels. The other approach—which I call confessional—would exhibit concurrently the credibility of the essential facts and of their Christian interpretation. It would invite the inquirer to assent to both in one indivisible act.

To illustrate the difference between these approaches, let us now turn to the resurrection of Christ. The historicist demonstration of this mystery is not lacking in logic. Reduced to a syllogism, it comes down to this: The Gospels are reliable historical sources; moreover, they affirm the bodily resurrection of Jesus; therefore, the bodily resurrection occurred. Since there can be no doubt but that the Evangelists mean to portray the resurrection of our Lord as both real and corporeal, neither the minor nor the conclusion can be challenged, provided the major is conceded. All that remains to be done is to reply to the objections.

Practically speaking, there are only four alternative theories. Some adversaries, like Reimarus, have held that the whole story was a deliberate fraud, but this is excluded by the manifest sincerity of the first Christians. Others, like Paulus, said that it was just a mistake: Jesus never really died, but fell into a trance from which He later revived. The Gospels, however, make it quite clear that the risen life was not a mere return to earthly existence, but a sublime condition, an initiation to heavenly glory. The third theory, that the whole story is a myth or legend, is refuted by the trustworthiness of the Gospels, which the historicist takes for granted at this point.

The most serious objection is no doubt the fourth one, namely, that the apparitions were hallucinations. But this objection too admits of an answer. How could the hallucinations have come to so many different witnesses on so many occasions, stretching over a period of so many days? Moreover, the risen Saviour was perceived not simply by one sense or even two, but by touch as well as sight and hearing. Besides, it is repeatedly affirmed in the New Testament that He ate and drank with His disciples—which implies that there would be enduring effects after His departure, such as an empty cup or a pile of fishbones. Finally, the hallucination theories do not account for the empty tomb, which is firmly attested by all four Gospels.

The conclusion that Jesus really rose from the grave is, on the foregoing grounds, asserted to be thoroughly evident. Since the argument has been conducted by historical methods, the conclusion may be called, in the language of the Scholastic manuals, "historically certain."

Now there is much in the arguments just summarized that is valid and should be retained. But to approach the whole problem with the presupposition that the Gospels are eyewitness accounts precise in every detail—this is to oversimplify the problem out of existence. It is to demand concessions which no adversary, nor even a well-informed believer, will grant. Once we consider the real nature of the Gospel narratives, certain difficulties begin to rear their heads.

First, it should be noted that the accounts of our Lord's apparitions which have come down to us in the Gospels are relatively late. Some of them are usually regarded as belonging to the most recent strata of Gospel material. For example, what appears in most editions as the finale of Mark (16:9–20) probably does not belong to the original text of Mark's Gospel. Whether written subsequently by Mark himself or by another writer, it shows signs of partial dependence on the other Gospels. The apologist cannot, therefore, appeal to this text as though it were a demonstrably independent testimony. The twenty-first chapter of John offers a similar problem. Critics usually regard it as an appendix to the fourth Gospel, very likely by a different hand. Many would ascribe it to the early years of the second century. This leaves us with only three accounts certainly attributable to the Evangelists themselves: those of Matthew 28, Luke 24, and John 20. We have practically no indications as to the prehistory of these pericopes before they became incorporated into the Gospels. We just know that they are there, in booklets written thirty to seventy years—some would prefer to say forty to eighty years—after the purported events. From a historian's point of view, this obviously creates a difficulty. Accounts composed so long after an event, which cannot be certainly traced to eyewitnesses, are far from ideal historical sources.

Secondly, we should remark that the three accounts are widely discrepant among themselves. Luke speaks only of appearances in and about Jerusalem, and so far as one can gather from his Gospel—prescinding from his further statements in Acts—all the appearances took place on one day, Easter Sunday. John in his twentieth chapter likewise reports only Jerusalem appearances, occurring both on Easter Sunday and on the first octave thereafter. Matthew, on the other hand, describes no appearances to the apostles except one occurring in Galilee an indefinite period after the crucifixion. His language seems positively to exclude any suggestion that Jesus appeared to the apostles in Judea. He represents the risen Jesus as telling the holy women to instruct the apostles to go to Galilee, where they would see Him. If the author of Matthew had known of Jerusalem appearances, would he have written his account in this way? It is very hard to harmonize the Galilean and the Jerusalem traditions. Many Protestant scholars hold that the Galilean appearances represent the earlier belief of the Church, and that the Jerusalem stories were a later expansion of the tradition.

The third difficulty relates to the literary genre of the resurrection stories. They fall into various categories. Some of the incidents are narrated in the concise, simple style characteristic of old, traditional material. But other episodes, such as Luke's account of the journey to Emmaus and the Johannine version of the lakeside apparition, are told with such consummate artistry as to suggest the hand of a skilled litterateur. Tales which had been handed down about half a century in the oral tradition would presumably be much simpler and cruder. In an important study of the Christophanies in the light of form criticism, Prof. C. H. Dodd argues that these highly circumstantial and literary accounts must be to some extent artificial constructions, influenced by dogmatic, apologetic, and liturgical motifs. He particularly notes the recurrence of the theme of the breaking of bread, which would seem to be an allusion to the Eucharist.

If the resurrection stories are late, difficult to harmonize with each other, and in some cases perhaps retouched by literary imagination, the apologist cannot base his arguments on the assumption that every detail necessarily represents a "hard fact." Whatever the ultimate conclusions of Christian biblical exegesis may be with regard to the factual content of these narratives, it may be questioned whether the sheer historian, using simply rational critical tools, can establish beyond doubt that Jesus ate boiled fish in the Cenacle on Easter Sunday or that He invited Thomas to touch His side when He reappeared the following week. An adversary will object that these details may have been inserted, not indeed capriciously, but for dogmatic rather than historical reasons. He will suggest that perhaps the Evangelists were seeking to inculcate, in opposition to any Docetist tendencies, the Church's doctrine that the risen body was physically real.

Such are some of the difficulties with which the historian is faced when he considers the New Testament data concerning the resurrection. When we honestly face these difficulties, we can begin to see why so many modern scholars have felt that the resurrection of Christ was something less than certain on historical grounds.

Before deciding whether history can demonstrate the fact of the resurrection, let us note at least that it can undoubtedly perform a very valuable service for apologetics. For one thing, sober historical investigation is able to exclude some of the more preposterous theories that have been advanced. It can show, for example, that the resurrection faith was not a late legend, formed under the influence of Oriental mystery religions. On the contrary, the conviction that Jesus had risen in body from the tomb was a central element of Christianity from the beginning.

The most cogent arguments to this effect are drawn not from the Gospels, which are admittedly rather late, but from the Acts of the Apostles and the Pauline epistles. The so-called kerygmatic sermons by St. Peter and others in the early chapters of Acts are generally held with excellent reasons to be representative of the earliest Christian preaching. The archaic terminology, the Semitic constructions, and the undeveloped theology in these sermons all indicate that Luke in writing them up is closely following very early sources, presumably Palestinian. These sermons clearly proclaim the physical resurrection of Christ as the very cornerstone of the Christian faith.

Still more important for our present purposes is the so-called Easter *paradosis* given by St. Paul in 1 Cor 15:3–7. Here St. Paul quotes—verbatim, it would seem—an early formula of faith which he himself probably learned before his baptism in Damascus or when he visited Jerusalem not more than ten years after the Crucifixion. In this confession it is affirmed that our Lord rose again on the third day in the very body which had been crucified and buried, and that He appeared to various disciples on several different occasions. In verse 11 Paul reminds his readers that this is the unanimous preaching of all the apostles. "Whether then it is I or they, so we preach and so you have believed." This attestation is irrefragable evidence that the Church in the earliest days confessed the real resurrection of Christ.

Can history take us one step further and affirm that the resurrection was not merely believed by the first Christians but that it really occurred? At this point we come up against a division of opinion similar to that already noted regarding the miracles of Jesus. Many historians hold that as men of science they are obliged to operate on the assumption that things have natural explanations. They will supply natural explanations to the extent that they can do so with verisimilitude. Where they cannot do so, they will simply confess that they have an unsolved problem on their hands. But in either case they will regard the real resurrection of a dead man as something too extraordinary, too contrary to the universal experience of mankind, to be admitted as a matter of scientific history.

The attitude of the unbelieving historian is well exemplified by David Hume. In the chapter "Of Miracles" in his *Essay concerning Human Understanding* he presents the following hypothetical case:

But suppose, that all the historians who treat of England, should agree, that, on the first of January 1600, Queen Elizabeth died, that both before and after her death she was seen by her physicians and the whole court, as is usual with persons of her rank; that her successor was acknowledged and proclaimed by the parliament; and that, after being interred a month, she again appeared, resumed the throne, and governed England for three years: I must confess that I should be surprised at the concurrence of so many odd circumstances, but should not have the least inclination to believe so miraculous an event.

In such a case, says Hume, he would simply deny that the sources were accurate. However improbable an error of this nature, it is less incredible than such a prodigious miracle.

Historians who reject the doctrine of Christ's resurrection most commonly maintain that the apostles experienced hallucinations of some sort. The theory can be proposed with some show of plausibility by a skillful advocate such as Loisy or Goguel. True, we tend to think of the apostles as robust and well-balanced men, capable of drawing the line between fact and fancy, but it must be remembered that they were in a situation of unusual stress. They were fatigued by the events of Good Friday, shaken by the sudden overthrow of their Messianic expectations, plunged into grief by the death of their beloved Master, trembling for fear of suffering a like fate. Under such circumstances they would have been more than ordinarily susceptible to parapsychological experiences. No doubt the discovery of the empty tomb cannot be easily reconciled with the theory of hallucination, but it must be remembered that this fact is first reported in the Gospels, written a full generation after the event. Is it not possible, then, that this story might be, as Bultmann puts it, a "late legend"? Or if one admits that the tomb was in fact found empty, for some reason or other, that very circumstance might have contributed to the excitement which precipitated the hallucinations.

There are, to be sure, a number of improbabilities in the hallucination-hypothesis. A profane historian would be mistaken if he thought it a neat solution, but he might be forgiven if, on his own postulates, he judged it more admissible than the hypothesis of a real resurrection.

Historians who accept the Christian doctrine will generally hold that scientific history has no right to deny the resurrection. But they do not necessarily affirm that anyone would be authorized in the name of pure history to maintain that the resurrection had occurred. Prof. William Albright, who is both a devout Christian and an eminent historian, has some very prudent reflections on the point in his *From the Stone Age to Christianity* (Baltimore: Johns Hopkins Press, 1946, p. 300):

What we have in [the Gospels] is . . . a reflection of reports of eye-witnesses who were overwhelmed by the profound experiences and the extreme tension of mind and body through which they had passed. Men who see the boundary between conventional experience and the transcendental world dissolving before their very eyes are not going to distinguish clearly between things seen in the plane of nature and things seen in the world of spirit. To speak of the latter as "hallucinations" is quite misleading, since nothing like them is otherwise known either to historians or to psychologists. Here the historian has no right to deny what he cannot disprove. He has a perfect right to unveil clear examples of charlatanry, of credulity, of folklore, but in the presence of authentic mysteries his duty is to stop and not attempt to cross the threshold into a world where he has no right of citizenship.

In affirming that history must stop short of affirming the resurrection, Albright raises a very grave question. Many Catholics are understandably uneasy at the idea of removing the resurrection from history. On the believer's view, is not the resurrection a historical fact? For the Catholic, at least, the resurrection was an objective occurrence. The body of Jesus left the tomb at a definite point of space and time. The apparitions of the risen Christ were not only spiritual experiences—as the language of Albright might seem to suggest—but also sensory phenomena, in which the real body of Jesus was seen by the bodily eyes of His disciples.

Yet we may perhaps concede that there is also a sense in which the resurrection is nonhistorical. It was not simply a return to the conditions of terrestrial existence but an assumption of Christ's body into eternal glory. His true dwelling since Easter Sunday is a realm not measured by space and time. The departure from the tomb was not seen by any man; perhaps it was invisible. Not even the apparitions were occurrences of a sort that fall within the normal controls of historical science. As Jean Guitton has written in his interesting study entitled *The Problem of Jesus* (p. 214):

> If an *historical* event is one that is verifiable universally, the apparitions do not belong to history. Though their object was one who had been known before his death by a vast number of contemporaries, the risen Christ never presented himself publicly to all, as he had done during his trial and Passion. History, in the strict sense, knows only events that are verifiable by any normal man and call for no privileged means of knowledge. . . . It would seem to me that if Tiberius or Tacitus, if Philo or Pilate or Josephus had happened to be present in that room where Jesus appeared, none of these would have seen anything at all.

In defense of this position Guitton can appeal with good reason to the New Testament. A careful reading of the resurrection accounts makes it clear that to see—or at least to recognize—the risen Jesus was a privileged form of knowledge, a special grace. In the tenth chapter of Acts St. Peter is presented as declaring that "Jesus appeared not to all the people but to witnesses designated beforehand by God" (v. 41). These foreordained witnesses were, according to the Gospel, the former disciples. And even these chosen witnesses did not easily identify Jesus in His risen form. Mary Magdalene mistook Him for a gardener. The disciples on the road to Emmaus first recognized Jesus after He had expounded the Scriptures to them, and in the course of a Eucharistic action. At the Sea of Tiberias it was reserved to the beloved disciple to perceive and to declare, "It is the Lord." The other disciples did not apprehend Him so clearly. Otherwise it would hardly be written of them that they did not dare to ask Him: "Who art thou?" (Jn 21:12).

These statements, taken collectively, reflect a tradition in the early Church that to perceive the risen Jesus required something more than the normal use of one's eyes and ears. The apparitions were mysterious events not open to common inspection. The disciples did not look upon Jesus with their bodily eyes alone, but with the help of a supernatural illumination. Their power of vision was fortified by the light of faith. In the profound expression of St. Thomas, the apostles "after the resurrection saw with the eyes of faith (*oculata fide viderunt*) the living Christ, whose death they knew as an evident fact (*quem mortuum sciverant*)" (*Sum. theol.* 3, q. 55, a. 2, ad 1m).

The style in which the apostles proclaimed the resurrection was entirely consistent with the mode in which they had learned it. If their conviction had been simply imposed by the evidence of the senses, they would perhaps have been tempted to convert others by adducing evidence of the same kind. But they were well aware that their own conviction was chiefly the result of an illumination from above. They appear before their fellow Jews not as reporters of a rare phenomenon but as heralds of a revelation. In their initial preaching—as summarized, for example, in the early chapters of Acts—they do not bother to state the details of how they have become convinced. Still less do they try to prove the fact by historical evidences. Instead they speak as authoritative witnesses. They announce the dogma as something to be accepted on their word as divinely appointed heralds. To be sure, they point to extraordinary signs such as the cures which they themselves work, but they do not try to deduce the doctrine from the signs. As men filled with the Holy Spirit, they prophetically interpret the true meaning of the signs. "Be it known to you all," says Peter, "and to all the people of Israel that in the name of Jesus Christ of Nazareth, whom you crucified, whom God has raised from the dead, even in this name does he [this former cripple] stand before you sound" (Acts 4:10).

Let us now turn from the Acts to the Gospels. Here we find a more detailed, circumstantial mode of statement. The narratives are fuller and more graphic. But still we have authoritative testimony rather than proof. The Evangelists are content to tell the story of Christ's risen appearance as known to the believing Church. The modern scientific historian will find grounds for complaining that the testimony is too late, too vague, too conflicting, too much influenced by doctrinal and liturgical motives, to be fully worthy of credit. More fundamentally, he will regard the very idea of the resurrection as something too outlandish to be accepted on the best testimony in the world. We have heard the sentiments of Hume on this point.

But if we change our perspectives from those of the profane historian to those of the religious inquirer, the evidence takes on a new aspect. By the religious inquirer we mean one actively seeking communion with God, eager for the tidings of salvation. The message of Christ's resurrection will not strike such a hearer as a merely bizarre occurrence, an interruption in the universal order of things. He will view the accounts in the total framework of the biblical story. God's action on behalf of His chosen ones, whom He redeems from suffering and crowns with glory, falls into a harmonious pattern. The total glorification of Christ, body and soul together, provides a fitting culmination to the religious history of ancient Israel. In the context of Pentecost, moreover, it takes its place as the foundation stone of a new, world-wide economy. The risen Christ, in sending forth His Spirit, inaugurates the final age of history. The resurrection, then, appears as the central event by which God offers hope of redemption from all the ravages of sin. Through the risen Lord the human race—and in some sense all creation—is restored to its pristine union with God. God becomes in Christ the author and finisher of salvation.

Seen in the perspectives of sacred history, the resurrection is a supremely meaningful event. It exhibits the loving-kindness of the God of Israel. Since it is revelatory and salvific, it may be judged fitting and possible. Fr. Levie, in the study already cited, makes much of the intimate bonds between dogma and apologetics. He points out (pp. 47 f.) how incredible the resurrection would be apart from its redemptive significance:

> If we bracket the doctrinal aspect, if we deny to dogma and theology any right to intervene in our apologetics, the resurrection of Jesus of Nazareth in April of the year 30 of the Christian era becomes an unintelligible fact, unthinkable to the human mind, since it would be meaningless and contrary to all ordinary likelihood. As a profane historian, I will have no choice except to reduce the documents which seem to favor it to the framework of the verisimilitude to which I am accustomed. . . . If my reconstruction runs up against serious improbabilities, they will seem to me more tolerable than a resurrection in which I can see no meaning.

The religious meaning of the resurrection gives it a certain prima-facie plausibility antecedent to any critique of the historical testimonies. Why, after all, should God not do an utterly singular thing here at this unique juncture of history, when the old Israel reaches its religious consummation and the new Israel is coming to birth? Might He not do for this transcendent religious teacher what He certainly would not do for Queen Elizabeth or Barabbas or Pontius Pilate? Once we have glimpsed the potential significance of the resurrection of Christ as a deed of God, there is less reason to frame desperate hypotheses, such as some unprecedented concatenation of collective hallucinations or some fraudulent legend of an empty tomb.

This reasonable anticipation of the truth of the resurrection solidifies into genuine credibility when we study the qualities of the apostolic testimony. All the criteria which point to authentic revelation, as set forth in the preceding chapter, are magnificently verified in the initial proclamation of the paschal mystery. It represents the unanimous faith of the infant Church. It is accepted without any shadow of doubt. Yet the event is one which, from all we can gather, contradicted the previous expectations of the apostles and their contemporaries. An isolated individual resurrection of the Messiah before the final consummation of the universe was something that would never have entered their minds. No wonder the disciples, as we see them in the Gospels, were amazed and bewildered at their Master's reappearance.

Finally, it should be noted that the witnesses of the resurrection were totally transformed by their experience. Face-to-face communion with the risen Christ fashioned them into new men. It made them slaves of the gospel, urgently compelling them to preach the glad tidings with power to the whole world. The Jews protested that this doctrine was blasphemy; the Greeks, that it was folly. But neither threats nor ridicule could reduce the apostles to silence. Whence came their conviction and the persuasive power of their proclamation? One explanation is that given by the apostles themselves, namely, that they have not believed lightly, since the risen Jesus Himself gave them full assurance of His triumph and of their mission to herald the good news. This explanation, if we accept it, fully accounts for the faith and proclamation of the primitive Church. Every other hypothesis labors under serious difficulties.

Historicist apologetics, I submit, has done a poor service in tearing the mystery of the resurrection from its theological context and setting it on the level of worldly prodigies. To some this approach has given a false sense of comfort; they have cherished the illusion that scientific history could virtually demonstrate this fundamental article of Christian faith. To others it has erected a formidable barrier, for it seemed to recommend detached investigation, conducted with the tools of profane history, as the ideal preparation for faith. Many conscientious persons, after sincerely sifting the data, felt obliged to admit that the precise occurrences can no longer be so easily reconstructed. In their assessment of the historical arguments these unhappy souls are perhaps more accurate than the advocates of historicist apologetics.

If we wish to experience the convincing power of the ancient testimonies to the resurrection, it would be far better to take our stand on the ground indicated by the New Testament itself. The accounts are religious testimonies addressed to believers or sincere inquirers. Men earnestly seeking communion with God can find in the Bible a solid warrant for belief. The religious meaning of the event itself, together with the extraordinary qualities of the apostolic proclamation, make it fully credible that Jesus did manifest to His chosen friends His new and glorious existence.

RECOMMENDED READINGS

K. Adam, *The Son of God*. New York: Sheed & Ward, 1934. The fine chapter on the resurrection (pp. 207–62) is still unsurpassed as a brief apologia.

J. Guitton, *The Problem of Jesus*. New York: Kenedy, 1955. Contains interesting psychological and philosophical reflections on the historicity and corporeality of the resurrection.

A. M. Ramsey, *The Resurrection of Christ*. 2nd ed.; London: Bles,

1946. A study by the present Archbishop of Canterbury valuable for showing the positions adopted by various modern Anglican and Protestant scholars. Substantially in accord with Catholic doctrine.

R. Russell, O.S.B., "Modern Exegesis and the Fact of the Resurrection," *Downside Review* 76 (1958), 251–64, 329–43. An excellent survey of the contributions of recent biblical scholarship.

★ 5 ★

The Divinity of Christ: History and Confession

In most current apologetics manuals the divinity of Jesus, like His resurrection, is a thesis to be proved. The main proof is very simple and runs approximately as follows. The Gospels, which are strictly historical documents, represent Jesus as claiming to be God. Further, they represent Him as authenticating His claims by miracles. Since God alone is the principal cause of any genuine miracle, and He would never miraculously seal a false teaching, it follows that Jesus' claims are true. Therefore He is God.

For present purposes let us grant, without conceding, that it can be conclusively shown through impartial historical investigation that Jesus worked authentic miracles. What do these miracles prove? Most rarely, if ever, does a sensible miracle, taken in itself, prove the wonder-worker to be God; he might be just an agent of God. For the success of the demonstration, therefore, it is all-important to show that Jesus claimed strict divinity.

Several different lines of argument are proposed to prove Jesus' divine claims. In general the manuals argue from the sayings of Jesus about Himself which are recorded in the Gospels. A series of texts are presented in which Jesus ascribes to Himself divine attributes or divine sonship.

The strongest texts are those from the fourth Gospel. In Jn 5:18, for instance, Jesus is said to have made Himself equal to God; in Jn 8:58 He claims strictly eternal existence ("Before Abraham was, I am"), and in Jn 10:30 He asserts: "I and the Father are one." In the Synoptics Jesus does not speak in such absolute terms, but He does refer to Himself as "Son" in a very exalted and completely singular sense. On several occasions, moreover, he seems to accept the designation "Son of God."

This customary mode of proving Jesus' divine claims must now be subjected to criticism. How does it stand up in the light of contemporary biblical studies? From what we have seen in previous chapters it should be clear that we cannot presume that the words placed on Jesus' lips by the Evangelists are exactly those which He uttered. Often they represent a further reflection on His doctrine, expressing how the Church in a later generation understood the mind of our Lord.

The problem of historicity is particularly acute with regard to John. It is a truism that the style and content of Jesus' utterances as reported by John differ markedly from what we read in the Synoptics. In fact, all the characters in John's Gospel, including even John the Baptist, speak in the same solemn, abstract, repetitious, hieratic style. "All these facts," as Feuillet remarks, "point ineluctably to the conclusion that John to some extent attributes to Jesus his own style of expression, while the Synoptics have retained the words of Jesus more literally in their original form" (*Introduction à la Bible* 2 [Tournai: Desclée, 1959] 670). The Johannine Gospel is in its way as historical as the others, but we cannot lightly assume that the discourse material in this one Gospel gives us the precise words pronounced by our Lord. Where John differs from the Synoptics, the latter are presumed to reproduce Christ's actual words more faithfully. We are, therefore, forced to rely principally on the testimony of the first three Gospels.

Even in arguing from these Gospels we must proceed with caution. It is important to keep in mind just what we are trying to do. We are not now asking whether there are in the Synoptics sufficient indications to satisfy a convinced believer that Jesus in His earthly life was fully conscious of His divine prerogatives. We are presently in the field of apologetics, not that of Christian exegesis. Our question is, therefore, whether the texts are sufficiently secure and unambiguous to persuade an unprejudiced non-Christian that Jesus claimed to be God.

The first fact to be noted is Jesus' great reserve in disclosing who He was. Never in the Synoptics is He represented as saying "I am God," or even "I am the Son of God." In a few passages others are reported as calling Him "Son of God" or asking Him whether He is the Son of God. Thus in the Marcan Gospel several demoniacs (3:11 and 5:7) recognize Jesus as Son of God, as does also the Roman centurion at the moment of Jesus' death. In Matthew Satan refers to Jesus as Son of God (4:3, 6), the apostles twice address Jesus by this title (14:33 and 16:16), and the high priest asks Jesus whether He is the Christ, the Son of God (26:63). Luke's use of the title adds nothing new except that the angel uses the title at the Annunciation (1:35).

In all of these instances Jesus never once accepts the title "Son of God" without qualification. He simply imposes silence on the demoniacs. When Peter calls Him Son of God, and when the high priest asks Him whether He is Son of God, Jesus replies evasively, substituting in His reply the term "Son of Man."

To this we may add that even supposing that these cases give us the exact words used (which may generally be questioned in view of the discrepancies among the three Synoptics), the speakers in question probably would not have meant Son of God in the strictest sense of that term. The idea that God would have a son by true and natural generation, equally sharing in His own divinity, would never have entered the mind of any believing Jew. Divine sonship in the Old Testament meant a relationship involving singular favor and intimacy with God. The term was applied to various created persons, and even to the Jewish people as a whole, who are collectively called the "first-born son" of Yahweh (Ex 4:22, etc.). Such usage makes it most likely that the term "Son of God" when applied to Jesus by other characters in the Gospel would have meant what would today be called some sort of moral sonship, that is, a relationship of very special love and familiarity.

This is not to deny that the Evangelists, when they use the expression "Son of God," are thinking of strict divinity. They are writing from the standpoint of a more developed faith and for the benefit of Christian believers. But it would be anachronistic to attribute to personages in the Gospel the same degree of understanding that the Church possessed some fifty years later.

The title which, according to all the Gospels, Jesus used by preference as His very own was "Son of Man." At first sight more lowly than "Son of God," it appears on examination to be the more exalted of the two. In the prophecy of Daniel (7:13) and in Jewish apocalyptic literature the Son of Man is a mysterious heavenly being closely associated with Yahweh. Yet not even the most avid devotees of the esoteric Son-of-Man literature would have supposed for an instant that the Son of Man was actually God.

Thus we cannot demonstrate the divine consciousness of Jesus from the titles which He used of Himself or allowed others to use of Him. We have to fall back on indirect arguments. The most forceful of such arguments is perhaps that drawn from the manner in which Jesus speaks of His relationship to the Father. While a few expressions attributed to Jesus in the Gospels would suggest a station of inferiority to the Father, others indicate something like equality. Thus, in a remarkable saying reported by Matthew and Luke, Jesus declares: "No one knows the Son except the Father, nor does anyone know the Father except the Son, and him to whom the Son chooses to reveal Him" (Mt 11:27; cf. Lk 10:22). The structural parallelism in this sentence seems to place the Father and Son in a relation of strict mutuality, and to oppose both to all persons who are not divine. It may, then, be interpreted as an affirmation of divine status. But are the words strictly historical? Do we have here the *ipsissima verba Iesu?* Quite possibly we do. We cannot rule out the hypothesis that the disciples may have overheard this reflection which Jesus is represented as making in His prayer, and have accurately remembered it. But the evidence of historicity is not so strong as to furnish a probative apologetic argument.

The principal difficulty against the historicity of this saying, and several others more or less comparable, is that if Jesus had spoken so clearly, it should have been evident that He claimed to be God. If so, no one could have become His disciple without admitting that He really was God.

But did the apostles, in Jesus' own lifetime, recognize

Him as a divine person? Many Catholic exegetes incline to a negative answer. Not even Peter in his most privileged moments seems to have come so far. Immediately after his confession at Caesarea Philippi, the prince of the apostles makes it clear that he still thinks of Jesus' Messiahship in political and nationalistic terms. He reproves Jesus and is in turn rebuked by Him. The conversation hardly betokens a recognition of Jesus' divinity. If we read the Gospels carefully, it becomes apparent that the disciples were very slow in overcoming this human and temporal concept of Messiahship. Even after the Crucifixion two of them are shown by Luke lamenting the passing of the Master who, as they hoped, was going to restore the kingdom of Israel (Lk 24:21). Now that He has failed to do so, they have lost faith in Him entirely. Writing in the symposium *Son and Saviour* (p. 75), Fr. Benoit says of the apostles:

> They needed time to appreciate even the fact that Jesus was the Messiah. And the very human way in which even then they interpreted his messianic role, the dullness of heart for which Jesus so often rebuked them, their scandal at the crucifixion, all of this makes it impossible to believe that they had any clear awareness of their master's divinity before their eyes were opened—and even then with difficulty—by the great miracle of the Resurrection.

The astonishment of the disciples at the resurrection and their reluctance to believe the testimony of the holy women and of their own eyes show that up to that time they had not thought of their Master as a divine being. Not even their dealings with the risen Jesus gave them all the light they needed. On the very day of His ascension, according to the first chapter of Acts, the disciples are still asking Him when He plans to restore the kingdom of Israel (1:6).

If it was not clear, even to Jesus' intimates, that He was

more than a national saviour, it may well be asked how a modern reader, by recapturing the words and actions of Jesus in His earthly life, could find a clear presentation of His divinity. As a factual historian, I suggest, he cannot hope to rise notably above the level achieved by Jesus' own disciples. As we saw in chapter 1, the chief aim of scientific historiography, as a positive discipline, is to reconstruct with maximum verisimilitude the phenomenal aspects of the past. The interpretive historian, to be sure, can go further, but his interpretation itself depends on tools other than those supplied by technical history.

Does this mean that academic history is useless in an apologetic defense of the divinity of Christ? Far from it. Historical research can show with great verisimilitude that Jesus in His earthly life gave numerous hints that He was more than an ordinary man, and that the secret of His personality was wrapped in an aura of mystery. Titles such as "Son of God," which He did not simply reject, and "Son of Man," which He used by preference, were well calculated to suggest that His origin was more than human, thus laying the foundations for a later belief in His divinity. While Jesus does not seem to have openly taught that He was God, He unquestionably sowed the seeds of that faith. The historian analyzing the Gospels can find many evidences that He must have spoken and acted in this way.

But to conclude that Jesus was, or even claimed to be, a strictly divine person would be to go beyond anything that sheer historical study can unearth. The historicist apologetic, to the extent that it undertakes to demonstrate this, has proved unsuccessful.

In previous chapters we have seen that to exploit the full apologetic value of the New Testament we must regard it not simply as a source of technical history but as religious testimony. Let us now consider how such an approach can illuminate the question of Christ's divinity.

The Gospels clearly exhibit the faith of first-century Christians that Jesus was a divine being, Son of God from all eternity. It is not difficult to show that such was the belief of the Evangelists themselves, both John and the Synoptics. In other books of the New Testament we have still earlier affirmations of the same faith. The epistles of Paul, written in the fifties and sixties, firmly profess this doctrine. Still earlier, it would seem, are the kerygmatic sermons which we find outlined in the opening chapters of Acts. Already in the sermon attributed to Peter on Pentecost, Jesus is identified with the Lord—the Adonai of the Old Testament—of whom it had been written that He would pour forth His spirit upon all flesh before manifesting Himself as universal judge at the end of time. In terms of the theological vocabulary available to Jewish Christians at the moment the Church was born, we could scarcely hope for, or even conceive, a more forceful affirmation of Christ's divinity.

Whence did the apostles derive their conviction that Jesus was Lord over all creation, sharing with His Father in the government of the universe? If we wish to accept the apostles' own account of their faith, we shall have to say that it was not simply a matter of assenting to what Jesus had expressly said of Himself in His earthly existence. Still less was it a logical inference from His miracles. Rather it was a religious insight following upon long familiar intercourse with Jesus. In His public life Jesus prepared the apostles for this tremendous truth. But the full realization was itself the fruit of Pentecost. It was by the light of the Holy Spirit, sent forth by Christ after His glorification, that the apostles came to understand who He really was. To penetrate the mystery of Jesus' person is never described as though it were the end product of human reasoning. "Flesh and blood have not revealed it to thee, but my Father in heaven" (Mt 16:17). In other words, to recognize the divinity of Jesus is primarily a matter of grace. "No one can say 'Jesus is Lord' except in the Holy Spirit" (1 Cor 12:3). The Holy Spirit, as we are told in the farewell discourse, will lead the apostles to know the whole truth about Jesus (Jn 16:13).

Since the apostles had not learned Jesus' divinity through sheerly external evidences, they did not seek to convince others by strict proofs. They gave no purely rational arguments from which Christ's divinity would follow as a necessary conclusion. Instead they pointed to prophecies and signs which were not in themselves probative. They themselves by their preaching gave authoritative interpretations of these texts and wonders. The heart of the kerygmatic sermons in Acts consists not in the force of the argumentation but in the power of the religious testimony. The same is true of the writings of Paul. As he says to the Corinthians: "My speech and my preaching were not in the persuasive words of wisdom, but in the demonstration of the Spirit and of power, that your faith might rest, not on the wisdom of men, but on the power of God" (1 Cor 2:4-5).

The Gospels, too, are essentially testimonies. They are written by believers with the expressed purpose that men may believe, or believe more deeply, that Jesus is the Son of God. The climactic statement at the end of the fourth Gospel (20:31) expresses the conviction that should result from a prayerful reading of any of the Gospels. The reader should join St. Thomas in his confession: "My Lord and my God!"

[69]

The great sign of credibility of this confession is, I submit, the apostolic testimony itself. The fervent conviction of the primitive Church, so bravely and powerfully heralded, stands out as a true miracle. Whence would the apostles have drawn their faith in Jesus' divinity if not from a revelation? How else can we explain that a group of pious Jews became so suddenly, so unanimously, and so unshakably convinced of a doctrine which to Jewish ears could only sound like blasphemy? It would be quite impossible to conceive that they would have exalted a mere man, one whom many of them had known in the flesh, to divine honors. In his strange and fascinating *Le mystère de Jésus* (Paris: Rieder, 1926, p. 84), P.-L. Couchoud eloquently shows that no such apotheosis could have occurred among believing Israelites:

> In many of the regions of the empire it was quite possible to deify a private citizen. But in at least one nation it was impossible, and that was among the Jews. They adored Yahweh, the one God, the transcendent and ineffable God, whose image they did not portray, whose name they did not pronounce, who was separated from every human creature by abyss upon abyss. To associate with Yahweh any kind of man at all would have been a sacrilege and a supreme abomination. The Jews honored the emperor but they let themselves be cut to pieces rather than profess even in a whisper that the emperor was a god; and they would also have let themselves be cut to pieces if they had been obliged to say the same thing of Moses himself. And would the first Christian whose voice we hear, a Hebrew son of Hebrews [St. Paul], associate a man with Yahweh in the most natural manner in the world? That is a miracle I refuse to accept.

In heralding the divinity of Christ, then, the apostles are proclaiming with full and unanimous conviction a belief which they could not conceivably have invented. This striking fact suggests the possibility that their views had been revolutionized by an actual revelation. When we look more closely at the doctrine itself, this hypothesis is magnificently confirmed. Contrary though it seems to all common sense, the doctrine of the Incarnation appears, on examination, completely worthy of God. It expresses to us, as nothing else could, the infinity of the divine love. It is the supreme and absolute manifestation of God's interest in the world which He has made. Once the doctrine is announced, it exposes the folly of assuming that God must conduct Himself as a simple spectator. Why should He not intervene when man needs His help? Since He created man with a capacity and longing for personal communion with Himself (as each of us can know from experience to be the case), it seems altogether likely that He might graciously satisfy that desire. If there is any view of God which is improbable and unacceptable, it is not the Jewish-Christian view of the God who saves; rather it is the deist view of a God who complacently stands aside. The "do-nothing" God of the philosophers—those who harden their hearts lest they hear the word of God—is the horrid coinage of a depraved mentality. If God were so cold and detached, it is impossible to conceive why He would have made the world in the first place.

Once we think in terms of the biblical concept of the God who powerfully comes to the help of His loved ones, we are on the road to a Christian vision of the universe. Christianity is simply the religion of the infinite God. We believe and confess the infinity of God's love for us, the boundlessness of His mercy and condescension. In giving us His own Son, He has made an infinite gift. The infinite charity of Calvary, the infinite sacrifice perpetuated in the Mass, the infinite elevation of man to a share in God's own trinitarian life, the infinity of eternal blessedness—all these infinities belong together. To a man who has once grasped the Christian out-

[71]

look on life, every other religious ideal looks pale and uninviting. Newman, it seems to me, was not far wrong when he wrote that there are only two completely consistent attitudes toward the world: one is Catholic Christianity and the other is sheer nihilistic atheism.

Considerations such as these exhibit aspects of the credibility of the Christian dogma of the Incarnation. They appeal to us, no doubt, if they felicitously formulate something that we ourselves have already dimly sensed. But in the last analysis the motives of credibility elude formulation. By an immensely complex assessment of a thousand converging factors we arrive at the persuasion that the doctrine can and ought to be accepted. At a certain stage in our meditations all the pieces fall into order and we see that the Christian proclamation is worthy of credence.

A cumulative argument of this kind is fully rational but does not lend itself to propositional statement. There can be no question of framing arguments, whether deductive or inductive, which rigorously prove the divinity of Christ. Syllogisms can have rhetorical and expository value, but they do not really recapture the dynamism by which the mind arrives at the recognition of Christ's godhead.

In closing, it may be helpful to recapitulate what I have tried to do in the preceding pages. I have discussed two basic methods of using the New Testament to establish the credibility of the Christian faith. One way, which I call the historicist apologetic, seeks to get behind the interpretation of the primitive Church and to show that the facts themselves, objectively considered, admit of no other interpretation than that which Christian dogma proclaims. This approach, in my view, is inadequate for two reasons. In the first place, the external facts, including even the words and works of Jesus, do not prove the truth of the Christian message in such a way that a coldly scientific investigator would feel obliged to assent. Secondly, we do not have any way of getting at the facts except through the testimony of the Church herself. That testimony, which is found chiefly in the Gospels, falls far short of what a scientific historian would consider optimum source material for the events in question.

The other method, which I have advocated as primary, is to treat the New Testament writings as religious testimony —a testimony embracing both factual memories and spiritual insights. The attributes of the testimony are such that the prudent man in search of religious truth can find it satisfying. The intrinsic sublimity of the message, its coherence, and its adaptation to man's religious needs make it eminently worthy of consideration as a revelation from God. The novelty of the message, and the conviction, unanimity, constancy, and spiritual power with which it was heralded, give us every reason to conclude that the apostles were the bearers of revelation. As men most intimately involved in the spiritual events of which they speak, they have an excellent claim to our trust.

The conviction that the Christian message is from God is not something we are forced to accept on blind faith. Our faith is a leap, but not a leap into the dark. It has a solid rational basis, and part of that basis is provided by the New Testament. But the New Testament is not simply the expression of an ancient faith. We read it today with full consciousness that the religion born with the apostles still retains its vitality. The witness of the primitive Church is enhanced by the witness of the Church today. The arguments from history thus ultimately rejoin the arguments based on the living reality of the Church: its marvelous propagation, its stability through the centuries, and its undying fruitfulness in all good works. In the last analysis, as Fr. Levie has observed, there are not many signs of credibility, but only one: the whole Christ in His Church. In apologetics these two together, Christ and His Church, should be viewed as a single sign, just as in dogmatic theology they are seen to be two facets of a single mystery.

RECOMMENDED READINGS

Son and Saviour. Rev. ed.; Baltimore: Helicon, 1962. Invaluable brief introductions to the testimony of Acts, Paul, the Synoptics, John, etc., on the divinity of Christ by Catholic scholars of the highest caliber.

L. Cerfaux, *Christ in the Theology of St. Paul.* New York: Herder and Herder, 1958. Good analysis of the Pauline texts on the divinity of Christ.

O. Cullmann, *The Christology of the New Testament.* Philadelphia: Westminster, 1959. A Lutheran work with a very fine analysis of the Gospel testimonies on Christ's claim to divinity.

J. Daniélou, S.J., *Christ and Us.* New York: Sheed & Ward, 1961. Chapter 2, "God Made Man," shows how the words of Christ, as reported in the Synoptic Gospels, amount to a claim of divinity. Much influenced by Grandmaison.

D. M. Stanley, S.J., "The Divinity of Christ in Hymns of the New Testament," *Proceedings of the Fourth Annual Convention of the Society of Catholic College Teachers of Sacred Doctrine.* Notre Dame: St. Mary's College, 1958, pp. 12–34. Accents the role of the Holy Spirit in the formation of the Church's Christological faith.

V. Taylor, *The Names of Jesus.* London: Macmillan, 1953. A work by an eminent Methodist exegete which gives valuable data on the various Christological titles in the New Testament, but is somewhat overinfluenced by the author's own theory regarding the evolution in Jesus' Messianic consciousness.

★ Index of Authors ★